The Challenge of Christian Marriage

———— ◇ ————

Marriage in Scripture, History and Contemporary Life

BY

THOMAS M. MARTIN

PAULIST PRESS
New York ◇ Mahwah

Library of Congress Cataloging-in-Publication Data

Martin, Thomas M., 1940–
   The challenge of Christian marriage: marriage in Scripture,
history, and contemporary life/by Thomas M. Martin.
      p. cm.
   Includes bibliographical references.
   ISBN 0-8091-3190-0
   1. Marriage—Religious aspects—Catholic Church. 2. Catholic Church
—Doctrines. 3. Marriage—Biblical teaching. 4. Married people—
Religious life. I. Title.
BX2250.M268   1990
261.8′3581′09—dc20   90-41233
                                    CIP

Published by Paulist Press
997 Macarthur Boulevard
Mahwah, New Jersey 07430

Printed and bound in the
United States of America

Contents

——————— ◇ ———————

Preface vii

1. Why Study Christian Marriage? 1
   Study Questions   8

2. Marriage in the Old Testament 9
   A. Marriage and Family in the Culture   12
      Family as a Source of Material Goods   16
      Family as a Source of Immortality   16
      Family as a Source of Identity   17
      Women and the Need for Family   18
      Styles of Marriage in the Old Testament   19
      Conflict and Divorce in the Family   21
   B. The Old Testament Theology of Marriage   22
      The Theology of the Creation Accounts   23
      The Theology of the Fall   26
      Other Theological Themes   27
   Study Questions   31

3. Marriage in the New Testament 32
   A. The New Testament Theology of Marriage   33
   B. The Family Image in the New Testament   40
      The Family of Jesus   40
      The Prodigal Son   43
      Rejecting the Family   44
      The Martha and Mary Story   45
   C. The New Testament Teaching on Divorce   47
   D. The New Testament Teachings About Children   48
   Conclusion   49
   Study Questions   53

4. Marriage in the Patristic Period **54**
   A. Two Basic Choices   55
   B. Adjusting the Intensity   59
   C. Addressing Marriage   61
   D. The Good of Marriage   64
   E. The Practice of Marriage   67
   Conclusion   69
   Study Questions   71

5. Marriage in the Medieval Period **72**
   A. Tensions Facing the Church   75
      Feuding Families   76
      Infanticide   77
      Nepotism   77
      Age of Marriage   78
      The Marriage Contract   81
   B. The Theology of Marriage   84
   Study Questions   91

6. Marriage in the Reformation **92**
   A. The Protestant Theology of Marriage   96
   B. The Question of Divorce   99
   Study Questions   102

7. Marriage in the Modern Period **103**
   A. The Unity of Human Life   103
   B. A New Perspective on Freedom and Emotions   106
   C. Sources of Change   107
   D. Two Basic Approaches   108
   E. Self-Centeredness, Marriage, and the Search for God   110
   F. The Family as Central   111
   G. The Specific Purpose of Marriage   112
   H. Specific Questions   116
      The Question of Divorce   116
      The Value of Sexual Expression   117
      The Scriptural Guideposts   117
   Conclusion   119
   Study Questions   121

8. The Christian Perspective's Challenge for Marriage **122**
   A. The Search for Intimacy   125
      The Christian Perspective   131

B. The Search Through Sexuality 133
The Christian Perspective 137
C. The Search Through Children 140
The Christian Perspective 143
1. Birth Control 145
2. Abortion 147
D. The Search Through Work and Creativity 149
The Christian Perspective 153
1. Domestic Work in Marriage and Family Life 154
2. Two Professional Careers in Marriage and Family Life 155
3. Single Career Marriage and Families 158
E. Marriage and the Stewardship of Wealth 160
The Christian Perspective 163
Study Questions 168

9. *The Theology of Christian Marriage* 170
A. Marriage as Part of God's Plan 170
B. The Need for God's Blessing 172
C. Marriage Creates a Sacred Bond 173
D. A Lifetime Commitment 177
Conclusion 178
Study Questions 180

10. *Conclusion* 181

For Brian and Shawn

———————— ◇ ————————

Acknowledgements

To write a text such as this requires that a wide range of areas be covered: scripture, specific historical periods, modern issues, and liturgy. It is always helpful to have people more versed in a specialty look over the shoulder to suggest this or that improvement. Joseph Kozar, S.M., Conrad L'Heureux, and Pamela Thimmes, O.S.F., were most helpful in making suggestions about the scriptural sections. William Anderson, Dennis Doyle, John McGrath, S.M., and William Roberts were helpful at different stages of the historical development. Norbert Burns, S.M., and Rita Bowen offered helpful suggestions in addessing the issues faced by Christian marriage today. Reverend Ted Bobosh and Reverend George Lytle were helpful in obtaining liturgical material.

Joanne Beirise was of great assistance in the preparation of the text as was Lisa Boone and my wife Mary Ann. Mary Jo Milillo worked on the preparation of the proofs.

Further acknowledgement should be extended to *Marriage and Family Living* magazine. Parts of the section dealing with marriage and work appeared in that publication, and the editor granted permission to use the material in this book. Alfred A. Knopf, Inc., also granted permission for the quote from John Cheever's "The Sorrows of Gin." Biblicial quotations are from The New American Bible.

Preface

——————— ◇ ———————

This study helps the adult reader understand the journey that the Christian community has traveled in its attempt to appreciate the richness and beauty of marriage. The journey starts with the treatment of marriage in scripture. Scripture is normative for most churches. It expresses the establishing revelation. When the faith community is seeking guidance through the thorny points of a given time in history, it goes back to this source for guidance. The trek to the scriptures is made with the full realization that both the Old Testament and the New Testament were expressed within the cultural settings of their day.

After looking at scripture, the journey takes what is for many modern readers a painful passage through the patristic period, a period which extends from about the second century to the eighth century and which gets its name from the male figures who led the church in its early years. The image of women as inferior, the sense of conflict between the physical and spiritual, and the grudging acceptance of marriage—all these attitudes which were so deeply ingrained in the mind of the period make it very difficult for the modern Christian to understand why the light of faith could not see through the limits of the day.

The study then focuses on the medieval period. The church of this period and that of the patristic age shared many of the same basic assumptions about human nature. As a result, the thinking about marriage did not undergo radical upheaval. However, what did change was the church's position in society. It was thrust into a position of authority as the one stable institution that survived the breakdown of the Roman Empire. As such it had to decide when marriage took place, what laws would govern its practice, what ceremonies would constitute marriage, and who would be allowed to marry. These questions which the church was forced to address led it to take a much more active role in the governing of marriage. During this period marriage was explicitly called a sacrament of the church, and all valid Christian marriages had to take place in the presence of an official witness of the church.

The reformation period which saw the growth of the Protestant movement found the marriage question swept into a whirlwind of many changes. Marriage was seen as a calling on a par with any other Christian way of life. It was also considered as a part of God's design for creation, but it was not placed as a sacrament of the church. The traditions that grew out of the Protestant movement argued that the sense of sacrament that characterized the medieval theologies was an aberration of the gospel message.

Finally the book looks at the modern tradition. First, the theologies of the different traditions today are examined. Then specific issues relating to marriage are examined in light of present Christian sensitivity. The study concludes with a study of the liturgies of different churches which should speak the heart as well as the head of the tradition. There are still differences between the churches in viewing marriage and the issues surrounding married life. Taken as a whole, however, the basic sense of marriage found in the celebrations of the different churches is remarkably consistent.

1.

Why Study Christian Marriage?

--- ◇ ---

It's early in the afternoon of the final day for class registration. Two roommates make an especially good match as they stand side by side in the twisting, disgruntled line. They are both engineering students. They are both comfortable in the sloppy apartment they call home. They both like to wait until the last minute to handle the necessities of life such as paying bills, washing laundry, and registering for class. This is the semester in which their tight-as-a-drum engineering program requires that they take a course from a list of liberal arts offerings dealing with human values.

They have both been looking at a course on Christian marriage. Both have some religious background. Their families went to church regularly. One of the roommates spent twelve years in parochial school. The other had only periodic religious education on Sunday mornings designed for those who attended the local public schools.

It looks as though the two will have about an hour and a half wait before they get to the registration window. The administration must have turned up the heat in the stuffy hallway as a way of punishing the procrastinators. To take their minds off their uncomfortable surroundings they discuss the pros and cons of taking a college course on marriage.

They both want to get married if they can find the right person. Not right away, of course. Perhaps after the first million. They are pretty sure of many things. They know how to balance the checkbook. They know how to talk and relate with the opposite sex. They know their way around the appropriate physical clinches. They know the meaning of commitment. For the last year they have made it a point to have dinner together every Wednesday night. Still they suspect that life with a spouse will be different than life with a roommate.

They have some idea about the dynamics of marriage from looking at their families. But the lessons there are not very helpful. One speaks of

1

how the grandparents are really cute together and seem to really be in love. But this older couple comes from another world. The parents are nice people. The old man is all right, but he lives in his own world emotionally. You never know what is going on inside. The mother means well, but she "overmothers." She constantly pressures others to do this or that. It seems as though the parents' marriage continues because they cannot think of anything else besides being together.

The other roommate relates how the grandparents were dead before the folks had any kids. The parents themselves are divorced. The only close model for a successful marriage is the older brother. Even his relationship has troubles. No, the sister-in-law and brother are not writing the script for a Harlequin romance.

Both agree that marriage is not easy and some preparation for this important future makes sense. But why the course in Christian marriage? They could just as easily take the one offered in sociology or psychology. The roommate with twelve years of parochial education relates how the religion high school marriage course was loaded down with a lot of boring details about what was necessary to make marriage proper. The teachers and text even tried to tell them how married people were supposed to act in the bedroom. There were indeed some ridiculous parts of that course. Sure, there were some good discussions about relationships, but at least half the course was a waste.

The other had some classes devoted to marriage at the church school. But everything seemed so removed from life. It seemed so wrapped up in the ideal with all those scripture quotes.

The more they thought about their past experiences, the more they hesitated in signing up for the Christian marriage course. They did everything but take their calculators out in an attempt to determine what elective they wanted. Sociology and psychology were ruled out on the basis of just how horrible the freshmen intro courses were. Perhaps the upper division courses were better. From talk around campus, however, they did not seem to light up many people's lives.

Other courses in the ethical field just did not seem to have much to do with their lives. The most convincing argument came down to the Christian marriage course's reputation. They heard of many who found it interesting; just about everyone saw it as a cake course. All lingering doubts, however, were obliterated when they saw that the only section offered fit perfectly into their slot between their two labs. It would be a great change of pace.

As they approached the registration window, both Jim and Sharon decided they would take the Christian marriage course. They were glad the decision was made. As they were congratulating each other on having that question settled, the elderly lady with the half-glasses hanging off the tip of her nose posted the most recently closed courses. Jim and Sharon groaned and quickly began to look through their options listed in the composite.

———————— ◇ ————————

The above vignette is not a particularly enlightening one in terms of why one should or should not take a course in Christian marriage. It is probably a fairly accurate scenario, however, of how many students go about choosing their courses.

In a sense the only reason why anybody should take a course, especially if it is an elective, is if the subject holds some promise of teaching about life. In the case of Christian marriage, one would presume that the course has something to teach about personal life.

What, however, does the Christian sense of life have that any good psychology or sociology course could not offer? That is not an easy question. It is not a question upon which all Christians themselves would find ready agreement. It is a question that will have to be addressed more thoroughly later in the book. In this introductory chapter, though, the best answer would probably be that Christianity offers a vision. It offers a set of glasses or a perspective which allows the individual to discover dimensions of life that can go unnoticed. In a sense a Christian would argue that marriage is changed when looked at through the community's vision.

Each of us looks at life through our personal experiences. A heavy-smoking, poorly conditioned man will not find an extended walk through any field a joyful experience. A woman attuned to bird watching will speak of meadowlarks, field sparrows, and kestrels. A farmer will speak of the size and health of the wheat.

Holmes Rolston brings out the importance of an individual's awareness in the following passage from his book *Science and Religion*:

"If I hadn't believed it, I wouldn't have seen it." Physicists spend decades looking for the neutrino. After repeated failures, they prepared extremely elaborate experiments (sixteen tons of scintillating liquid, 144 photomultiplier tubes, electronic apparatus 120 feet long) finally to catch it—inferring it from rare flashes of certain kinds amidst thousands of other flashes, arranged for with hundreds of thousands of dollars' worth of equipment, all taken two miles underground in a South African gold mine.

On the other hand, when physicists got a theory that suggested that they look for positrons, they looked back to discover that positrons had been appearing for years in cloud chamber photographs and ignored as an anomaly. One can't see what one isn't looking for, even though the evidence is amply present. Often what we find ourselves looking *at* depends on what we are looking *for* and *with*.[1]

Science, therefore, is not a simple discipline that looks at the observable facts and reports the physical realities. It is a study that requires scientists to have not only sharp eyes but also keen minds. Investigators must not only observe and collect data to formulate theories; they must also formulate rich theories to allow them to observe the data. In a sense the theory serves as a lens or a prism that brings to light or to focus different dimensions of reality.

Unlike a given popular mindset that thinks of ideas as being right or wrong, scientists are much more tolerant toward theories past and present. Any respectable theory probably has proven either effective in manipulating the physical world or at least efficient in accounting for observable phenomena. A theory is replaced when old data can be accounted for by a simpler explanation or when new data arises. The new data offers a different set of challenges which in turn cries out for a different set of explanations.

One author captures the tentative nature of scientific theory in the following terms:

> According to quantum mechanics, a subatomic particle is not a particle like a particle of dust. Rather, subatomic particles are "tendencies to exist" . . . and "correlations between macroscopic observables" . . . They have no objective existence. That means that we cannot assume, if we are to use quantum theory, that particles have an existence apart from their interactions with a measuring device. . . .[2]

Scientific theories, then, are like religious visions in that both are interpretative tools. They are different, however, in what they investigate and in what they accept as evidence. The first deal with observable data and are offered in response to contained phenomena. Religious views, on the other hand, address not only what is present but what should be present according to normative convictions. Scientific theories generally test themselves by the observable facts. Religious convictions, on the other hand, try to address the inner realities of the individual person and the ulterior design of human nature and of the world.

Certainly religion must make adjustments to accommodate for changes in human society and advances in the experience of the world. There is usually the conviction in the religious vision, though, that the change is a growth and development of the original vision and not a complete change.

Perhaps one moves a little closer to the nature of religious vision with the idea of an historical interpretation. Unlike scientific theory, historical interpretation must enter the realm of human motivation and intention. It must ask why people behaved the way they did. Part of the answer to this question comes in clearly observable events—the floods occurred, the army with its artillery was stronger, the two peoples had a long-standing animosity. Frequently, however, the events are not that clearly articulated. Frequently, the hierarchical importance of the events is not that easy to determine because one must deal with the human factor.

William H. McNeill, for example, argues in his book *Plagues and Peoples* that the Spanish conquest of Central and South America is such a startling event that it supplied him with the thread necessary to unravel many of the other mysteries of human history. A handful of Spaniards under Cortez was able to overthrow the powerful Aztec empire centered in Mexico City. That, in itself, is startling. But what is even more difficult to comprehend is that Pizarro carried out a similar feat against the Incas in South America. When lightning strikes twice, one must carefully ask why.

Does the historian center on the greater technology of the Spaniards? Does the focus shift to the clever way that the Spaniards fit into the existing myths of the Amerindians? Should the stress be placed on the potential hostility of conquered tribes within the confederation which the Spanish could so readily use for their own designs? Can any single factor be isolated as far more significant than the others?

These are not questions that permit an easy answer. Probably they are not even questions that permit a single answer. Every now and then, however, an historian comes along with a fresh interpretation that weaves together the evidence and the conjecture so convincingly that it causes everyone to take a fresh look at human events.

McNeill, for example, centers his interpretation of the Spanish conquest on the diseases that they introduced to the new world. Once he flushed out his perspective in that region, he then saw that disease played a key role in every theater of human drama. He does not argue simply that disease was important in this or that historical movement. That is an obvious point that certainly was not missed by previous historians. What he was arguing was that the movement of disease is the single most important factor in accounting for the ebb and flow of human struggles.

He presents his case in the following terms:

The lopsided impact of infectious disease upon Amerindian popula-
tions therefore offered a key to understanding the ease of the Spanish
conquest of America—not only militarily, but culturally as well. But
the hypothesis swiftly raised other questions. How and when did the
Spaniards acquire the disease experience that served them so well in
the New World? Why did the Amerindians not have diseases of their
own with which to mow down the invading Spaniards? Tentative answers to such questions soon began to uncover a dimension of the past
that historians have not hitherto recognized: the history of humanity's
encounters with infectious diseases, and the far-reaching conse-
quences that ensued whenever contact across disease boundaries allowed a new infection to invade a population that lacked any acquired
immunity to its ravages.

My conclusions will startle many readers, since events but little
noticed in traditional histories assume central importance for my account. This is because the long line of learned scholars whose work it
was to sift surviving records from the past has not been sensitive to the
possibility of important changes in disease patterns.[3]

Like the scientist, then, McNeill discovered new data. More accu-
rately he became aware of data that had been given secondary or tertiary
importance in isolated events. He wove the data together to show how it
deserved central stage in understanding the dynamics of human history.

The end product brought a rush of "brilliant's" from the reviewers
because of the insightful way it accounted for so many details and movements. But this interpretation, indeed any interpretation of history, will
never become as paradigmatic as a central theory in science. The data of
history is simply too multifaceted, the reality too complex. One is dealing
with a plethora of cultural, economic, political, and military events that
all interplay with the interior makeup of a people.

Likewise, historical theory differs from religious vision. It tries to
determine what happens. It tries to determine how humans interacted
with the determined events. It does not try to present what should happen, nor does it try to account for any ulterior reality or design in its
attempt to determine what happened. Religious convictions, like historical theories, must take into account the events of human history as they
are known. They must also adjust their vision by what is discovered to
be the case in fact. However, most people with religious convictions feel
they have an unwavering insight into the secrets of human life as it is
anchored in the mysteries of the ulterior design of reality.

Religious groups do differ in just how specific they feel their knowledge of the ulterior design is. Some feel that their knowledge of the

world's fate approaches what in ordinary language could be termed factual. Others would speak of their knowledge of the ulterior design more in terms of insight or inscape that the tradition has into the mystery of reality. It is an insight that must continually dialogue with the present culture as both learn from each other.

Within Christianity, those who speak of their grasp of the world in more factual terms would be considered fundamentalists or conservative. Those who are more open to learning from the culture because God is seen as ever active in the world would be known as liberal. Most mainstream Christian groups have within their own church or community people who lean in either direction. In both cases, however, they see their faith tradition as having much to offer people who want to enter into such a basic human relationship as marriage.

It is the purpose of this book to help articulate what the Christian vision of life together would be. The study will begin in the next chapter with a look at scripture. The Bible is considered normative for any Christian vision of life. The following chapters will address the historical development of the Christian tradition as it tried to remain faithful to this scriptural norm while participating in a variety of significantly different cultures. Such an historical perspective is necessary to understand how the church arrived at its present understanding of marriage and to appreciate how it deals with the movements evident in our present society.

After this historical survey, the study will then move to the practical questions facing modern marriage and try to specifically address how the Christian perspective offers insight into what is taking place and what should take place.

Finally, the work will close with a look at the marriage rite contained in the Christian tradition. There is probably no better way to articulate the Christian ideal of marriage than to look at the initiating ceremony with which the two people begin their life in marriage.

NOTES

1. Holmes Rolston, *Science and Religion* (New York: Random House, 1987) p. 10.

2. Gary Zukov, *The Dancing Wu Li Masters* (New York: William Morrow, 1979) pp. 215–16.

3. William H. McNeill, *Plagues and Peoples* (Garden City, New York: Anchor Books, 1976) pp. 2–3.

2.

Marriage in the Old Testament

———————— ◇ ————————

Christians consider the scriptures normative for their sense of reality. True, the Old Testament and the New Testament comprise a body of literature that represents a very limited understanding of the earth, of the makeup of physical reality in general, and of certain dimensions of human nature. But it is also a literature that represents the conscious reflections of a people with a unique experience of God.

The Jews before Jesus and those who had the Jesus experience reflected on their lives in light of their experience of God. Christians feel that this God experience and its implications for human life are so profound that it is normative for their community. True, the vision must be weighed against what has been learned through the centuries, but it cannot be dismissed.

Many people, of course, reflect on their experience of God, and through this effort they gain valuable insight into human efforts and destiny. Vatican Council II in its "Declaration on the Relationship of the Church to Non-Christian Religions" states that the church must respect the truth of other religions:

> She looks with sincere respect upon those ways of conduct and of life, those rules and teachings which, though differing in many particulars from what she holds and sets forth, nevertheless often reflect a ray of that Truth which enlightens all men.[1]

Given this respect that most Christians feel for the activity of God in other religions, in creation, and in the activities of human events, Christians still give an honored position to scripture. They feel that God was uniquely active in human affairs during the formative years of the Bible. In particular they see the Jesus event as so fundamental to any realization of life that subsequent religious reflection must weigh itself against what was brought to light by Jesus' words and actions and the experiences of those who had immediate contact with Jesus or his disciples.

Any reflection on Christian marriage, then, must start with an appreciation of what is said about marriage and family in scripture. At first that task may sound easy enough. However, there are significant complications simply because the experience of family life is so culturally conditioned. Family deals with the very fabric of a people. It is going to be steeped in the practices and the sense of reality of the day.

Many of the practices of the early Jews are simply scandalous when measured by what is acceptable today. In the Old Testament the conflicts within the most important families, the treatment of women, and the way the individuals drew their identities from the group are quite baffling to a person living in present western culture. Similarly, in the New Testament the apparent dismissal of domestic life takes many readers' breath away.

From the very beginning, then, a distinction must be made between the cultural practices of the day and the theological reflections that the people made on their experience. The two are not unrelated, of course, but they cannot be assumed into one. The theological reflection is clearly influenced by the practices of the day. Likewise, the practices of the day can be seen to change ever so subtly as the people reflect on their experience of God. Nevertheless, there is a tension that exists between the style of life that the religious sense of reality called forth and what in fact was the practice of the people.

Likewise, there must be a distinction between the immediate theological conclusions that are drawn by a people and those which stand the test of time. In the Old Testament, for example, many times the Israelites justified their savage treatment against their enemies by appealing to the revenge of God. In the New Testament, on the other hand, the early Christians were taken up with an apocalyptic vision in which they expected the risen Jesus to return to the earth within their lifetime to establish a radical new order. The modern reader of the Bible cannot make sense out of either of these theological underpinnings.

The Christian, then, listens to the Bible, but it must be critical listening. There must be an appreciation of how the Israelites and the early Christians were transformed by their experience of God. There must also be an awareness of how their own peculiarities caused these people to formulate their response according to the dictates of their own culture.

The Old Testament covers a considerable expanse of time. Some significant figures and their approximate dates as set by modern scholarship indicate just how wide a scope of time the Old Testament encompasses:

Abraham—1600 BC

Moses—1275 BC

Joshua—1225 BC

Samuel—1025 BC

David—His reign lasted from 1005 to 965 BC

Solomon—His reign extended from 965 to 926 BC

Northern Kingdom—Lasted from 926 to 722 BC

Southern Kingdom—Lasted from 926 to 587 BC

This chapter is obviously limited in what it can say about the origin and nature of the Old Testament. However, some sense of its scope is necessary to appreciate the primitive ways of family life reported in most of the books as well as the changes in life seen throughout its development.

What must be realized is that for most of the history of the Israelites nothing was written down. They were an oral people. The different tribes that came to identify with the Israelite nation had their own versions of the founding covenant which they passed down from generation to generation. None of the material was written down until about 950 BC. Actually the process was a complex one in which different oral versions were consolidated into different written versions. In turn numerous written versions were woven into consolidated forms.

The process was finalized in the middle of the sixth century of that era with modern scholars identifying four main traditions in the first five books—the Pentateuch—of the Old Testament. These earliest books are important for understanding the remaining books of the Old Testament. They capture the founding traditions against which later developments are measured.

The four traditions of the Pentateuch are called the Yahwist tradition, the Elohist tradition, the Priestly tradition, and the Deuteronomic tradition. These traditions present the earliest reflections of the Israelites on their family lifestyle. As they think about their family in light of their experience of God, the Old Testament people undergo a long, tortuous journey. Any change that takes place is not a question of a dramatic breakthrough in which God laid down the laws and practices that were to govern how a husband and wife were to deal with each other. There were no simple handbooks on how to raise children.

A. Marriage and Family in the Culture

One who has grown up in a culture where family is seen primarily as a community of intimacy simply finds life in the Old Testament rather raw and shocking. Perhaps the family reality that most experience is far from ideal. However, the ideal that is expressed in television stories featuring families such as the Huxtables (*The Cosby Show*) and the Keatons (*Family Ties*) shows what we would like our families to be. In a sense they indicate what many in our society measure their experience of family life against. The shows may be recognized in part as unrealistic; however, they are not simply dismissed by their faithful audiences. The repeated experience of the close and warm families raises a good number of sighs and secret longings in those who watch. Somehow the shows touch on what could be. Perhaps they call to mind what is—at least in imperfect form—in the present family lives of the viewers.

Even the harsher television stories with the Ewings (*Dallas*) and the Carringtons (*Dynasty*) do not measure against the gritty reality of family life in the Old Testament. Perhaps a few case studies will bring the point home more dramatically. The following are examples of some of the family situations found in the Old Testament. They are presented in a "Dear Abby" format. Read the case and think about your response before moving on to how Solomon unravels the drama according to life in the Old Testament.

Case One

Dear Solomon:

My wife has not been able to get pregnant. I have done everything I can. We desperately want children since without them we are nothing. What should we do?

Signed,
Abe

Dear Abe:

Since your wife is obviously being punished by God and will probably never become pregnant, your only course of action is to take a concubine and have children by her. I would suggest you talk your wife into the idea and have her pick one of her maidservants. That will ease the potential jealousies that are bound to develop.

Signed,
Solomon

Case Two

Dear Solomon:

I was given to the master of the household to have children for the family. When my time comes, I am supposed to sit upon the lap of the wife, Sara, and allow the child to pass through her legs so she can claim the child as her own.

I am willing to be used this way; otherwise, I may never have children and my life will be for nought. However, I cannot tolerate the abuse that the wife heaps upon me. She is driven by a blind jealousy at my good fortune. She hates me because God has looked upon me with the favor of a child. I am about ready to run away even though I have little hope for sustaining myself or my child. I just cannot bear her continual cruelty to me.

Signed,
Hagar

Dear Hagar:

First, realize that part of the problem may stem from you. Do not act in a haughty way, flaunting your fertility and blessing in front of your mistress. Life is difficult enough for her since God has seen fit to punish her by depriving her of children.

Second, do not run from your master and mistress. Tolerate your suffering and God will bless you. You will have so many kids you will not be able to count them all.

Signed,
Solomon

Case Three

Dear Solomon:

My family has been disgraced. Last week in the town square in Sodom I met two men who were travelers. I offered them the hospitality of my house for the night. They accepted.

As you know, our city is not known for its morals. All the men of the city, both old and young, came to my door demanding that I cast the visitors out so that they could have their sexual pleasure with them. I had offered these visitors the mantle of my hospitality. My family honor was at stake. I would have done anything to avoid such a shame being brought on the name of my family. What could I have done?

Signed,
Lot

Dear Lot:

You should have thrown your two virgin daughters out to the

crowd. That might have contented the mob and saved the honor of your family. It would at least have been worth the try.

Signed,
Solomon

Case Four

Dear Solomon:

We have had a difficult life. We lived in that cesspool of human debauchery, Sodom. Life there was difficult enough. People were such animals. One night our father, on the advice of some screwball seer, even tried to throw us out the door to a mob of lustful idiots. He tried to explain how we must be willing to sacrifice ourselves to the good of the family and its honor.

Our situation is desperate now. Sodom was destroyed by a fire-storm. Our mother was turned into a pillar of salt because she looked back with fond memories at what was in Sodom. As a result we are now living in a cave with our father. There is no hope of our getting married and having children. Who would want us in our impover-ished, filthy condition?

Please help us. We cannot face the prospect of virtually having no identity. Without a family one is nothing.

Signed,
Daughters of Lot

Dear Daughters:

It sounds as though you have a Lot on your mind. The only solu-tion I can think of would be to get him drunk and sleep with him so that you might become pregnant. It would not improve your immedi-ate situation. It will give you some brighter hope for the future.

Signed,
Solomon

Case Five

Dear Solomon:

My husband, Er, displeased the Lord and was slain. My father-in-law, Judah, realized that he had the sacred obligation to provide one of his other sons to fulfill the levirate obligation to carry on Er's name. Accordingly he sent his second son Onan to have intercourse with me so that the children could be considered as the offspring of Er and carry on his name.

Onan did not want his own children to be deprived of some of the inheritance. Therefore, he wasted his seed upon the ground before we would have relations; and I was not able to have children by him. God saw the injustice and slew Onan.

At this point Judah got rather nervous. He had already lost two sons. He blamed me in some way. He was not about to send me his third son, Shelah. His excuse was, at first, that Shelah was simply too young. He promised to have him fulfill the sacred levirate obligation once he achieved sufficient physical maturity. Meanwhile, I was sent back to my family of origin where I am considered little more than a lowly servant. I have no husband. I have no children. I have no hope.

What should I do?

Signed,
Tamar

Dear Tamar:

I would suggest that your only course of action lies in seducing or tricking either of the two remaining males of your husband's family. From what you have told me, I see little hope of an honest seduction. They do not look upon you kindly. However, they have a duty toward the memory of Er. Some trickery might be in order.

Try disguising yourself as a prostitute and see if you can win one of the men to your bed. At your age, you'd better concentrate on the father. When you begin to show with child, you'd better be prepared for the floodgates of fury. However, if you can prove that you were impregnated by your father-in-law, I believe he will be shamed enough at neglecting the levirate obligation that he will leave you be in peace and not stone you to death.

Signed,
Solomon

Case Six

Dear Solomon:

I am getting desperate. When we first got married, God blessed me with children. He kept my husband's other wife barren as a punishment, for Jacob loved her and not me.

Life was fine. Even though my husband did not love me, I was able to get respect because I was the only one bearing children. Rachel, however, was not content to abide by God's will. She gave her maidservant to our husband. The maidservant started to bear children. Then for some strange reason God permitted Rachel to bear children. I am losing my position of honor in the family. What should I do?

Signed,
Leah

Dear Leah:

    If you find yourself temporarily unable to bear children and you are losing your place of honor to the other wife, I think it is time for some action. Go to your husband and demand that he take one of your maidservants to bed so that you also may claim a child through your maidservant.

Signed,
Solomon

These examples are drawn from the first book of the Old Testament, Genesis, and give a good flavor of the Semitic life upon which the Old Testament sense of family was based. The Abraham and Sarah story is taken from the sixteenth chapter of this book. It illustrates how important family was to these people. They would do literally anything in order to have family. They had no developed notion of an afterlife. This life was the only dance they had to do. Family therefore fulfilled many functions.

Family as a Source of Material Goods

As God's chosen, the Israelites expected to be blessed if they obeyed the will of God, but this life was the only one in which to receive blessings. They therefore thought of material goods. They wanted large herds, many tents, and other signs of material prosperity. In that sense they were enthusiastic materialists. The key to understanding their emphasis on family is to realize that family was pivotal to all other blessings. It supplied the workers and the fighters that in turn provided prosperity and security.

Family as a Source of Immortality

There were other functions of family. Besides the material benefits of a large family, particularly a large family of males, there were the more existential benefits. In the absence of any viable afterlife, family was the only source of immortality. With children, the bloodline could in some way continue to exist. The father and mother would also be assured that some people would tell their stories. The memory of the parents would live on.

Living on in the memory of your offspring may not sound like an exciting sense of immortality. If it is the only game in town, however, one must participate or face the reality of extinction. One's family tree will come to an end without children. There were in their sense of reality no other alternatives to the family if one wanted any continued existence.

Most people today find the idea of dying without leaving any children a difficult reality to face. Yet many choose not to have children, and others simply are not able to have any. While a childless life is not without its trials and difficult decisions, the trauma is muted to some extent because we are such strong individualists. Family is important, but the basic unit of identity for people today is the individual.

There is a fluidity to the modern setting that allows people to become oriented in a variety of human experiences. The sense of the natural has been blunted in a technological world. Products are made to meet immediate demands. Similarly, human relationships or communities can be built to meet the demands for belonging and roots. Besides, the majority of the population has either a vague or a developed notion of personal immortality in which their spirit will live independent of the body. With such an alternative there is not as desperate a need for a continued presence in this physical life.

Family as a Source of Identity

The Old Testament did not have any developed notion of the spiritual immortality of the individual. Toward the latter part of the Old Testament period, around the second century BC, there was some sense of continued physical life after death centered around the resurrection of the body. However, belief in the immortality of the soul, so common in society today, was inherited from the Greeks and adopted by the Christians in the first few centuries of the present era. The Israelites of the Old Testament could not think of themselves apart from belonging to the earth and belonging to a people. Throughout most of the Old Testament era, family was needed not only for some sort of immortality but also for a sense of identity in their earthly life.

This concept of a family, a clan, a tribe, a nation is not all that easy to unpack for the modern mind. There were a number of realities that overlapped. There was the *beth'ab* or "house of one's father," the *go'el* or sense of family solidarity, the *mishpahah* or motive of the clan, and the *shebet* or tribe. The nuclear family was obviously not isolated from the larger association of relatives. In fact the lines were not always that easy to distinguish. But the nuclear family was the basic unit. It was the foundation.

Abraham and Sarah's actions indicate that one must try different

avenues to have children. Their days saw the practice of modified monogamy. There was only one wife; but at least when the wife was
barren, concubines could be employed. In a ritual in which the pregnant
woman sat on the knees of the man's wife, the child was claimed to be
the offspring of the main couple.

Women and the Need for Family

The story also intimates the dire position of women who faced a life
of barrenness. The more children a woman had, the greater her prestige.
This social reality is what motivated Hagar to flaunt her belly in front of
her barren mistress. It also gave her the energy to face the cruel punishments thrown her way by the enraged Sarah. The prestige that comes
with children also explains the motivation behind some of the other
stories.

The competition between Rachel and Leah (Gen 30) is an intense
battle for more and more children in which they employ the efforts of
their maidservants Bilhah and Zilpah. Their peculiar form of rivalry
makes sense only to the extent that one understands the importance of
children in the lives of these women. Similarly, Lot's seduction by his
daughters is completely incomprehensible unless the reader makes an
effort to enter their world. Women faced a life without identity if they
could not find some way of getting children.

When a woman was left in a family without husband and without
offspring, as was the case with Tamar (Gen 38), she was left with nothing. When a later book of the Old Testament, the book of Ruth, tried to
preach a sense of undying loyalty to a kin, one got a glimpse of just how
dire was the life of an unwed woman without offspring. Ruth refused to
abandon her mother-in-law even though her own husband and her
father-in-law were deceased. There were no immediate males to offer
the two any hope. Ruth was forced to glean grains from the field. In
other words she had to go out and pick up the droppings after the
harvest in an attempt to keep herself and Naomi, her mother-in-law,
from starving. Only after a distant male cousin consented to take the
women under his protection was there any hope that life might take a
more positive turn. The book is clearly trying to teach that those who live
a life of sacrificing love will be rewarded by God. However, within the
context of the day, God had to work through the good intentions of a
male to show how Ruth was rewarded for her efforts.

Perhaps no story depicts the dire position of women better than the
story of Lot and his concern with the honor of the family's name. Just
before the destruction of Sodom and Gomorrah (Gen 19) the messengers

from God come to the town to warn Lot and his family. He does not recognize them as coming from God, but he does offer them the graces of his home. Once the blanket of hospitality was extended, the family was responsible for the well-being of its guests. If somehow the guests were mistreated, the family was disgraced. Likewise, if the family was disgraced, all in the family were disgraced.

Family identity explains part of Lot's actions in the story. By itself it does not account for Lot's willingness to cast his daughters to the crowd. He probably would not have been willing to throw out his sons, if he had had any, to the mob's pleasures. No, one must appreciate the lowly position of women to understand Lot's behavior.

A woman was always under the control of a man—her father, her brother, her husband. From the point of view of the marital relationship the husband was called the "master" or *ba'al* of his wife (Ex 21:3; 22:2; 2 Sam 11:26; Prov 12:4), and in places the married woman is called the possession of her master (Gen 20:3; Dt 22:22). The control of the male was so extensive that the husband could nullify vows made by his wife (Num 30:10–14).

Styles of Marriage in the Old Testament

The marriages of the Old Testament run the gamut from modified monogamy, seen in the Abraham and Sarah story in which concubines were permitted, to polygamy and practical monogamy. Obviously with Jacob, Rachel, and Leah, the Israelites practiced polygamy. Polygamy was recognized as a legal reality in Deuteronomy (Dt 21:15) and later in the Talmud which limited the king to eighteen wives and the commoner to four. A survey of such books as Proverbs, Ecclesiastes, Song of Songs, Wisdom and Sirach, however, would seem to indicate that the monogamous marriage is presumed.

The movement toward monogamy may be the result of simple practical considerations. Large families were an important asset when one lived a nomadic lifestyle. They were an economic liability for one who was a craftsman living a settled life in a small town or village. The other force moving the people to the practice of monogamy may have been the growing sense of what marriage is in light of their experience of God. The impact of the God experience on marriage practices will be addressed more thoroughly later in this chapter.

At any rate, the woman was, by modern standards, at the will of her husband. While there were few restrictions on his sexual behavior, there was no question of her fidelity. It was through her that the purity of the line was guaranteed. The women were strictly watched and controlled in their dealings with men outside the family.

The laws governing extramarital relations and rape are helpful in realizing the importance put upon the woman's fidelity. If a married woman was found to have had relations with another man willingly, she was to be put to death. When Judah found out Tamar was pregnant, he fully intended to put her to death until she proved that she had relations with him in an attempt to have offspring. When a rape of a married woman or one betrothed took place within the city walls, both the woman and the man committing the crime were to be stoned. The man's fault was that he did not respect the rights of another family. The woman's fault was that she did not resist with her very being when there was a possibility that the attack could have been overheard and stopped (Dt 22:22–24). If, however, the rape took place in the country, only the man would be executed since there was little hope that the woman in her distress could be heard by others.

On the other hand, the laws governing the sexual relations of a single woman show a concern for protecting the woman as well as the rights of the family. Originally the law (Ex 22:15–17) stated that in the case of sexual relations with an unmarried woman, the man was forced to pay the value of the daughter to the father. The father then had the option of forcing the man to marry the daughter or not. The reform in Deuteronomy 22:25–27 stated that once the fifty shekels were paid to the father, there was no choice. The man had to marry the woman and was not permitted to divorce her.

It is not easy for people today to see how the provisions of Deuteronomy are a reform in an effort to give some protection to the woman. The woman was given no choice. Conceivably she could be forced to marry a man who had raped her. What woman would want to marry such an individual? Secondly, why tie the hands of the father who would want to seek a better marriage for his daughter?

These questions simply show how foreign the cultural practices of the Israelites really are to the modern experience. Certainly today a woman would not want to marry someone who raped her. Marriage today is for personal reasons. We marry for love. We marry to form a community of intimacy. Besides, a woman who is raped has a good deal of trauma to face, but she does not become an anathema to other men.

By contrast, the Israelite woman lost any prospects of a decent marriage once she was raped. She was used, and usually only desperate men would even consider such a woman for a wife. As for taking the decision out of the father's hand, one can get a clue as to why the reformers would do so from Lot's treatment of his daughters just prior to the destruction of Sodom. There were probably fathers who loved their daughters deeply and considered them daddy's little girl. In the culture, however, this deep parental love was not the norm. Women were a point of bargaining for a family. Their relationship with their father was not primarily one of personal intimacy. Conceivably what the reformers were trying to avoid were the many fathers who would take the initial money from the men guilty of the rape and then try to strike whatever bargain they could elsewhere with little or no regard for the well-being of the daughter.

In short, from the woman's perspective, any marriage was preferable to a life where one remained single and without offspring. Secondly, as the story of Leah shows, marriage to someone who loved you was preferable, but intimacy was not the primary reason for family life. If a woman could find some marriage that would bring her an element of prestige, she took it.

Conflict and Divorce in the Family

Once married, of course, the woman was not all that secure. She could easily be divorced. The governing text for divorce is the opening verse for Deuteronomy 24. A man may divorce his wife if "he finds in her something indecent."

The passage is rather vague and clearly leaves itself open to a variety of interpretations. Lawyers today would have a field day with a term as open as "something indecent," and in fact the Old Testament period saw its range of interpretations. In the rabbinical age of later years there were two main schools. The followers of Shammai admitted divorce only for "adultery and misconduct." The followers of Hillel "would accept any reason, however trivial, such as the charge that a wife had cooked a dish badly, or merely that the husband preferred another woman."[2]

With the possibility of the husband resorting to such trivial cases as those proposed by the school of Hillel, one can appreciate just how tenuous a woman's position was in married life. The only way to find some security beside the obvious luck of being given to a compassionate man was to have children. Motherhood cemented her bond to the family. It raised her esteem in the community. It increased her worth to her husband.

The emphasis on the value of children to the mother, so evident in the Rachel and Leah competition, should not conjure up scenes of a woman tenderly caring for her offspring and in turn being nurtured in her old age by those who addressed her every wish. Undoubtedly such realities existed at least in muted forms. But again the modern person must stretch the imagination to try to get into the reality of family life as experienced in the culture of Israel. Family was primarily an economic and social unit for the Israelites.

The general tone of family life reported throughout the Old Testament is one of conflict, jealousy, and struggles—I against my brother, my brother and I against our cousins, my brother, my cousins, and I against the world. That sequence would be one way of capturing the underlying attitude of Jewish family life. The books are filled with sibling rivalry. Cain slays Abel (Gen 4:8); Jacob blackmails Esau as the older brother is at the point of starvation (Gen 25:31); Joseph is sold by his brothers into slavery (Gen 37:25–28); Amnon rapes his sister Tamar (2 Sam 13:14). Similarly, relations between parents and offspring are often at odds. The classic story is found in Rebecca favoring Jacob over Esau. She ruthlessly plots with her favorite to trick Isaac in his old age. She wants Jacob to gain the blessing of the first-born (Gen 27).

Most of the stories of parent and sibling hostilities single out the father-child conflict. The father was, after all, the dominant parent, and the conflicts would naturally focus on him. Similarly, the celebration of children was often done in terms of the joy they brought to the father (Pss 127; 128).

The bottom line is, however, that there is ample evidence of how important children were for women in adding stability and honor to their lives.

B. The Old Testament Theology of Marriage

The previous section investigated what the overall practice of family life was in the cultural setting. As explained in the beginning of this chapter, that is only one consideration. A specific look at how the Israelites reflected on their experience of God is important. More to the point of this study, it is important to consider how the reflection in light of their God experience, how this theology, caused them to ever so subtly change their ways of behavior. At the very least it should have changed their ideals of behavior.

There is no doubt that the Israelites were conscious of God active in their lives. The stories related in the first section spoke readily of God choosing who would be fertile and who would not be. Modern explanations, obviously, would look to other causes. For the Israelites, God was directly responsible for everything. He certainly was responsible for the most important reality in their lives—their families.

The Theology of the Creation Accounts

One place where the influence of their religious experience is evident is in the beginning of the Old Testament. Chapter 1 of Genesis gives the creation account as presented by the priestly tradition. Chapter 2 presents the Yahwist tradition's version of how the world was created.

The priestly account was probably written in the sixth century of that era by the priests of the southern kingdom. It reflects the theological position that benefited from centuries of experience and growth in their appreciation of God's calling. From the point of view of marriage, the important verses are Genesis 1:27-28.

In the first of these two verses there is a play on words. Translation from the original texts to English is not easy; however, most interpretations agree that somehow the play on words is designed to capture the complementarity of the male and the female. The New American Bible translation presents the verse:

> God created man in his image;
> in the divine image he created him;
> male and female he created them.

This particular translation shifts from the singular masculine pronoun in the second line to the plural in the third line. It captures how the species is one, but the one species is not complete without both the male and the female. There is no attempt at this point to establish any hierarchy.

By implication, therefore, this sense of complementarity and equity is the way that God intended the relationship to be from the beginning. This is the ideal. There is no hint that the two are not equal in the original design. The harsh reality that was in fact the life of the Israelite women was not the way things were intended.

Some may argue that the sense of equity in the text is not that evident. They may insist that at best it is implied. However, if this and the second creation account are interpreted in light of the curse after the fall, it becomes evident that the author of this creation account is indeed presenting the two species as equal. The story of the fall, which will be discussed in the next section, clearly shows that the inequality of the sexes in the life of the Israelites was a punishment that resulted from the fall and was not intended by God from the very beginning.

Verse 28 of the first chapter continues by addressing the marital relationship more directly:

> God blessed them, saying: "Be fertile
> and multiply; fill the earth and subdue it.

> Have dominion over the fish of the sea,
> the birds of the air, and all the living
> things that move on the earth."

Obviously, marriage is presented as God's plan to increase the human race. Since the human is made in the image of God, as verse 26 asserts, then it is logical that the human is meant to be the dominant creature on the earth. The human is called upon to take charge of creation.

Such a charge may cause people steeped in the modern experience to cringe. They have seen humans gobble up huge portions of the earth to the point where other life forms are threatened. It is quite possible that before the end of the century there will not be any wild elephants, tigers, lions, or pandas left on the earth. And these are just the more dramatic examples of how other life forms are threatened by human presence.

If the creation account were written today, it might well urge humans to live in harmony with the ecosystem. But just as many of the experiences of the Israelites are difficult if not impossible for us to comprehend today, so this modern reality could not have been foreseen by the writers of the first creation account. They were dealing with a people struggling to make their presence felt in a world that was quite overwhelming. The modern experience is not the Jewish experience of the sixth century BC.

Turning attention to the second chapter of Genesis, the creation account from the Yahwist tradition is of much older origins. The God here is a more simple, homey type. Where the God of the Priestly tradition goes around and gives commands only to see cosmic powers come into being and take their ordered places, the God of the second creation account must go about his task on a much simpler scale. When he wants to make man, he must work with a hunk of clay. He formed the figure of a man and then breathed into the nostrils. The clay sat up and looked around.

What followed is not without its touching humor as the story pictures a man who after the initial excitement of creation becomes lonely. God in an attempt to relieve this loneliness begins forming all types of wild creatures, presents them to the man, and allows the man to name them.

This naming process concurs with the first creation account which commanded that humans were to have dominion over the earth. Those who had the power to name had the power to control. God, in allowing the man to name the products of his creation, was giving the human creature the power to rule over other creatures.

The humor of the second creation account is caught in the unsuccessful attempts. God had intended to relieve the man's loneliness. His attempts were in vain. The most he was able to cull from the man was a mild interest as the creature would pass on a weak compliment and a name when the hard-working God would show the results of his latest effort. Finally God got an idea. He would try to stimulate his lethargic prize of creation by making a creature similar to the man but with important differences. Man's reactions verify that finally God got it right. Verse 23 reports:

> "This one, at last, is bone of my bones
>   and flesh of my flesh;
> This one shall be called 'woman,'
>   for out of 'her man' this one has been taken."

The following verse then goes on to address the passage that has the most direct application to marriage. It is the passage that will be quoted in the New Testament. It is the passage that forcefully shows how the two must form a close unity:

> That is why a man leaves his father
> and mother and clings to his wife, and
> the two of them become one body.

The sense of complementarity, the sense of bonding, the sense of unity is stronger here than in the first account of creation. Some commentary from conservative groups will stress that since man came first, he is the prototype and is meant to have the place of honor. Some liberal commentators, on the other hand, have argued that since the woman was made last, she is the perfection of man. Both cases seem to be arguing their causes rather than taking the passage as presented.

As found in the text, there is a clear presentation that the two in the marriage become one in some fundamental way. There is a bonding that goes beyond simple social custom, personal intentions, or practical design. There is a unity that grows out of the very nature of human existence. The couple must think of themselves in unison and not simply as two individuals who have entered into a contract.

Both creation accounts, therefore, present a strong message about the dignity of male and female. Both stress the unique relationship of husband and wife.

This, then, is the explicit theology of the two creation accounts. The key message is the same. The expression does vary to some extent. But there is another important theological point made in the creation accounts which may not be too evident to the modern reader. It is a central point, however, and a sore spot in the continued history of the Israelites.

Although marriage is seen as involving a special bonding which calls upon the spouses to think and live as though they are one, it is not pictured as in any way opening the doors to special epiphanies. It is not an avenue for tapping into the sacred powers of the divine as so many of the fertility cults would insist. On the contrary, creation itself was holy. Creation itself was a part of God's handiwork, and marriage was placed in the context of creation taken as a whole.

Israel was frequently tempted to imitate the practices of the people who surrounded them and turn the sexual experience itself into a special religious ritual. Humans experienced such a powerful expression of life in the sexual act that they felt they were breaking into sacred time and space. But the Old Testament continually calls its people to place the end and goal of marriage within the universal call of creation. In a sense one could say that sexuality and marriage were secularized.

The Theology of the Fall

With such a beginning, then, how did the realities of Israelite life come into being? How could women be treated so lowly? How could the marriage bond be treated so lightly with polygamous marriages and with the ease of divorce? What happened between the creation accounts and the practice of family life in the remaining parts of the Genesis account?

In a sense the clash between the ideal presented in the creation accounts and the realities of Israelite life cannot be understood unless one realizes that the creation accounts represent the considered religious reflection of a people who have had many centuries to mature. In a sense, the creation accounts are saying: This is what marriage should be. This is what the relationship of male and female should be. This is what was intended by God from the very beginning, from the moment of creation.

As a text, the Bible links this ideal intended by God from the very beginning to the realities of Semitic life by reporting the fall from the ideal. In other words sin comes into the picture. Humans do not live up to the ideal. Adam and Eve disobey God and are in turn punished by him in proportion to their guilt.

The tradition generally sees the story of the fall presenting the woman as having the greater guilt since she is pictured as leading the man into the sin. When the punishments are meted out, it is not surprising, therefore, that the woman receives the greater sentence.

Eve receives a threefold punishment. She is now to bring forth children with intense pain. She is still going to lust after her husband only to find herself with child again. Finally, the male will be her master. In other words the ideal set up by God has been disrupted.

Such a typography is not surprising given the patriarchal structure of the society. In a sense the mandate that the literature had was twofold. It had to justify the given practices of the society. That is a function that myths and the sacred stories of a people fulfill. Secondly, myths and the founding stories of a people are supposed to stretch them toward an ideal.

The theologians working with the creation accounts could not simply condemn the traditional way of life of its audience. They did, however, want to challenge the practices of the day. Their solution was to present the ideal as the original order and to present the fall as the alternative order. The effect of this strategy, in all probability, was to strengthen a growing sensitivity among the people for the need to treat each other with love and respect.

Other Theological Themes

Against the reality of Semitic family life, one finds celebrations of marriage that capture in some degree the ideal presented in the creation accounts. In other words, despite the effects of sin, there developed a sense that marriage was a moving, unique bond. The language and the images used clearly indicate that there was a more powerful force active in marriage than was recognized by the legal realities of Israelite life.

One finds in the Song of Songs a sensual celebration of passionate love that pushes aside the legalities of divorce and the conflicts that dominate the families found in the Genesis account. Here the unity of the couple is captured through the sensuous bonding of the love.

The bride sings out to her beloved:

> Let him kiss me with kisses of his mouth.
> More delightful is your love than wine!
> Your name spoken is a spreading perfume.
> That is why the maidens love you.
> Draw me! (1:1–4)

Later in the first chapter, one of the responses of the groom is to praise the beauty of his spouse:

> To the steeds of Pharaoh's chariots would I liken you, my beloved:
> Your cheeks lovely in pendants, your neck in jewels.
> We will make pendants of gold for you, and silver ornaments. (1:9–11)

There may not be, in truth, many girls today who would be swept off their feet as their loved one compares them to a horse. Every culture has its images that excite them. But such language exchanged by men and women capture in some way how on a sensual level, at least, Israel senses how taken a man and a woman can be with each other.

On another level one finds the marriage bond being given the utmost compliment by comparing the relationship of marriage to the bond between God and Israel. The experience of God and Israel was not an easy one, but it was an enduring one because no momentary unfaithfulness can undo the bond between them:

> The Lord calls you back, like a wife forsaken and grieved in spirit,
> A wife married in youth and then cast off, says your God.
> For a brief moment I abandoned you, but with great tenderness I will take
>   you back.
> In an outburst of wrath, for a moment I hid my face from you;
> But with enduring love I take pity on you, says the Lord, your redeemer.
>   (Is 54:6–7)

The context of the statement is Israel's constant unfaithfulness. There are times when God becomes angered and turns his back, but the love is an enduring one which cannot be broken by the infidelity of the partner. God always relents and accepts his bride back into the good graces of his love.

The implications for the marital bond is obvious. It is a relationship that should not be taken lightly. Perhaps marriage can never live up to the ideal offered by the faithfulness of God. Still, the challenge of the ideal should serve marriage well.

Similar passages that compare the marital relationship and the domestic life to the love Yahweh has for Israel can be found in other parts of the Old Testament. Jeremiah 2:2–32, Ezekiel 16, Ezekiel 23, and Hosea 1–3 are some examples.

In fact these comparisons were probably introduced to draw upon daily life to emphasize just how good and faithful God was. The practical effect of the comparison was not simply to impress upon the people how dependable God was. In reality the comparison served to raise the Israelite appreciation of the beauty of marriage. The contrast is dramatic between the following quotes taken from both ends of the Israelite tradition.

In the laws of marriage taken from the book of Deuteronomy the twenty fourth chapter reads:

> When a man, after marrying a woman and having relations with her, is later displeased with her because he finds in her something indecent, and therefore he writes out a bill of divorce and hands it to her, thus dismissing her from his house: if on leaving his house she goes and becomes the wife of another man, and the second husband, too, comes to dislike her and dismisses her from his house by handing her a written bill of divorce . . . then her former husband, who dismissed her, may not again take her as his wife after she has become defiled (Dt 24:1–4).

By contrast one reads in the prophet Malachi the following passage which shows a significant change in the sense of commitment in marriage:

> Did he not make one being, with flesh and spirit:
>   and what does that one require but godly offspring?
> You must then safeguard life that is your own,
>   and not break faith with the wife of your youth.
> For I hate divorce, says the Lord, the God of Israel,
> And covering one's garment with injustice, says the Lord of hosts;
> You must then safeguard life that is your own, and not break faith.
>   (Mal 2:15–16)

There are many experiences which cause this significant shift. Somewhere in the measure of events, the comparison of marriage to the bond existing between Yahweh and Israel must be measured.

Actually the honored comparison for marriage must be placed in a larger picture. In the last line of the quote from Malachi, one reads the phrase, "and not break faith." Throughout the Old Testament an important theme is the sense of covenant.

There are several covenants or agreements mentioned in the Jewish scriptures. They signify an agreement or a bonding that exists between God and his people. A covenant is not like a modern contract in which people confront each other with different sets of obligations. In the contract, if one of the parties fails, then the contract is voided. By contrast, the covenant between Israel and Yahweh was a generous bonding initiated by Yahweh. He accepted Israel despite its continued unfaithfulness. This is the sense of commitment which had its impact on the thinking of marriage in the Old Testament. It will also have its impact on the thinking in the Christian era.

NOTES

1. "Declaration on the Relationship of the Church to Non-Christian Religions," section 2, in *The Documents of Vatican II*. Walter Abbott, ed. (New York: America Press, 1966) p. 662.

2. Roland de Vaux, O.P., *Ancient Israel* (New York: McGraw-Hill, 1961) p. 34.

STUDY QUESTIONS

1. Why is scripture considered normative for all subsequent Christian communities?

2. Why was family so important in the Old Testament?

3. Why are the creation accounts so important for understanding the development of the Old Testament view of marriage?

4. What were the different styles of marriage in the Old Testament?

5. What are some of the practices of the Semitic family that are difficult to understand by the present culture?

6. What was the attitude toward divorce in the Old Testament?

FURTHER STUDY

de Vaux, Roland. *Ancient Israel* (New York: McGraw-Hill, 1961). Gives a sense of marriage customs and the position of women and children.

Martin, Thomas M. *Christian Family Values* (New York: Paulist Press, 1984). A readable book that devotes two chapters to the family in scripture.

Pedersen, Johannes. *Israel: Its Life and Culture* (London: Oxford University Press, 1926). A dated study, but one that gives an excellent sense of the Semitic family.

Schillebeeckx, Edward. *Marriage* (New York: Sheed and Ward, 1965). Excellent for developing the theology of marriage in scripture.

Swidler, Leonard. *Women in Judaism* (Metuchen, New Jersey: Scarecrow Press, 1967). A readable study of the subject.

3.

Marriage in the New Testament

—————— ◇ ——————

The previous section on the Old Testament tried to show how the experience of God stimulated a very gradual change in the family life of the Israelites. The sense of sacredness in life that their experience of Yahweh created could not help but have an impact on their sense of how husband and wife were to treat and to consider each other.

The New Testament inherited this tradition of the Old Testament. However, the translation was not an easy one. In the Old Testament the experience of God was persistent, but it did not match the dramatic, all-absorbing experience of God in the Jesus event. The sense of God's pending activity was so intense among the earliest Christians that everything in daily life paled in its light.

The New Testament spans only a few decades. It does not show the gradual change in family and marriage. In fact, most of its books do not focus in any direct way on marriage and family. Where there is reference to marriage and family, the passages usually are attempting to drive home the all-important message of preparing for the kingdom of God which the early Christian expected to be established within their lifetime.

It would make little sense then to try to glean what were the customs of marriage and family during the times of Jesus. He did not spend time trying to reform the practices of the day. His presentation for the most part bypassed the practices of daily life and challenged his listeners to a radical conversion.

This present section, therefore, will be organized differently than the previous one. Where the treatment of the Old Testament looked at the customs of the Semitic people and then examined how the experience of God caused gradual but important changes, this section will go more directly to the theological reflections. Comments will be made on the customs of the day where these provide an appropriate context for understanding the nature of the New Testament challenge.

A. The New Testament Theology of Marriage

Perhaps the best way of understanding how the early Christians incorporated the heritage of the Old Testament into their thinking about marriage is to look at a passage from Ephesians 5:

> Wives should be submissive to their husbands as if to the Lord because the husband is head of his wife just as Christ is head of his body the church, as well as its savior. As the church submits to Christ, so wives should submit to their husbands in everything.
>
> Husbands, love your wives, as Christ loved the church. He gave himself up for her to make her holy, purifying her in the bath of water by the power of the word, to present to himself a glorious church, holy and immaculate, without stain or wrinkle or anything of that sort. Husbands should love their wives as they do their own bodies. He who loves his wife loves himself. Observe that no one ever hates his own flesh; no, he nourishes it and takes care of it as Christ cares for the church—for we are members of his body.
>
> For this reason a man shall leave his father and mother,
> and shall cling to his wife,
> and the two shall be made into one.
>
> This is a great foreshadowing; I mean that it refers to Christ and the church. In any case, each one should love his wife as he loves himself, the wife for her part showing respect for her husband (Eph 5:22–33).

It is difficult for readers today to appreciate the endearing relationship that is pictured here. The elevated position given to men is obvious and offensive to those whose daily life is a struggle for an appreciation of their true worth as women. However, if one can understand the patriarchal structure of the society, the passage can then be appreciated for how it moves the relationship of husband and wife to a new level because of the Jesus event.

In the previous section the covenant theme was seen as playing a central role. God conferred his help, or he graced the world with his presence and commitment. Jesus was seen as the final covenant by the Christians. He was seen as the final graceful presence that would permanently transform the world.

Where the Old Testament compared the marriage bond to that of the covenant that existed between God and Israel, this quote compares the marital bond to the relationship that exists between Christ and the church. If the wife is to submit to the husband, it is not business as usual for a patriarchal society. The model used is Christ. The husband is therefore expected to respond in kind. They are to exhorted to "love your wives, as Christ loved the church."

Probably the passage has limited pastoral use today because of how serious the patriarchal issues are for marital relations. In the future, if the community grows sufficiently, perhaps it can more easily appreciate how this comparison called Christians far beyond the normal practices of the day. The relationships are transformed as they are moved to the level of relationship experienced in Jesus.

Theologically, the passage has been important. Marriage is placed at the heart of the mystery of God relating to the world. After quoting the second creation account in verse 31, the text goes on to explain that this bonding of husband and wife is the foreshadowing of the bond between Christ and the church. The New American Bible translation quoted here uses the word "foreshadowing" in verse 32. Other translations use the term "mystery" while earlier Catholic editions would follow the Vulgate edition and use "sacrament." At any rate marriage is seen as in some way symbolizing or capturing the essence of God's activity in the world as fulfilled in Jesus' relationship with the church.

In strong contrast to the passage from Ephesians, one finds a startling statement about Christian marriage in the first letter to the Corinthians. In chapter seven of this epistle, St. Paul presents a jolting passage. It flies in the face of the Old Testament thinking and shocks the sensibilities of many present day Christians. The passage reads:

A man is better off having no relations with a woman. But to avoid immorality, every man should have his own wife and every woman her own husband. The husband should fulfill his conjugal obligations toward his wife, the wife hers toward her husband. A wife does not belong to herself but to her husband; equally, a husband does not belong to himself but to his wife. Do not deprive one another, unless perhaps by mutual consent for a time, to devote yourselves to prayer. Then return to one another, that Satan may not tempt you through your lack of self-control. I say this by way of concession, not as a command. Given my preference, I should like you to be as I am (1 Cor 7:1–6).

Not only is this passage difficult for modern day Christians, but it was equally difficult for the Jews of the day. It serves clear notice that one faces in the Christian message a call for a radical change in life. Everything lost its importance in the presence of God's impending action.

In the first sentence, the advice that a man is better not having any sexual relations is almost incomprehensible in light of the Jewish tradition. The previous section showed how everything revolved around the family. The Jews considered themselves as God's chosen people. They expected to give obedience to God, and in return they expected to be blessed. However, this life was the only one for which they could gather much enthusiasm. Therefore, they expected to be blessed in this life, but family was the key to all other blessings. It was the source of immortality, prosperity, security, and identity.

The previous section showed how desperate both men and women were if they could not have a family with an appropriate number of offspring. To the people who identified with the main line of Jewish tradition, Paul's opening words of advice would be all but incomprehensible.

True, there were Jewish groups around the first century of this era who reflected the mystical influence of other religions. Greek religious traditions in particular with their dualistic sense of life had some impact on small groups in Palestine. The dualistic view of human life saw two parts in conflict—the spiritual part and the physical part. The spiritual part was the important one and had to be nurtured over the physical part.

But the overall Christian message certainly did not fit into a dualistic pattern. It does not present the physical and spiritual dimensions of human life as in conflict. In fact the largest portion of the New Testament remains thoroughly Jewish in that it could not conceive of human beings in anything but physical terms. When it presented a sense of an afterlife, it spoke of the resurrection of the body and not the immortality of the soul.

There were other Jewish fringe groups which had picked up on what is called an apocalyptic vision. Such a view of life sees the present order coming to an end and a new time being established in which life will be changed in ways so radical as to virtually defy human imagination. The Christian message has more in common with these religious movements.

The Christians were expecting Jesus to come in glory within their lifetime. He was to establish a radical new order that was described by Matthew in the following passage:

Immediately after the stress of that period, the sun will be darkened, the moon will not shed her light, the stars will fall from the sky, and the hosts of heaven will be shaken loose. Then the sign of the Son of Man will appear in the sky, and "all the clans of earth will strike their breasts" as they see "the Son of Man coming on the clouds of heaven" with power and great glory. He will dispatch his angels "with a mighty trumpet blast, and they will assemble his chosen from the four winds, from one end of the heavens to the other" (Mt 24:29–31).

Christianity did share its call for a radical lifestyle with other groups that had Jewish roots. But the Christian message was primarily intended for the mainstream Jewish audience. For these Jews the message would not be easy to take or to understand. For these people, marriage and family were so deeply ingrained in their life that every male was legally charged to marry by a certain age.

Paul's opening sentence is indeed startling when placed within the mainstream Jewish culture of the day. His passage does not dismiss marriage and family as bad. This is clear in his second sentence. In fact he counsels most Christians that they should marry. But his presentation of marriage as almost a concession to the weakness of the average person fails to celebrate the Jewish enthusiasm for the family.

Paul's vision of marriage is not dripping with idealism. The purpose of marriage, in rather blunt terms, is to avoid immorality. Paul speaks of the "conjugal obligation." It is a rather curious term for today's audience which has such an appreciation for the beauty and the value of physical love. Did you do your "conjugal obligation" today? What a strange mentality. And in truth the New Testament attitude about marriage and family is strange for modern readers be they Christian or the curious.

Given Paul's situation, however, it did make sense. He was writing his letter advising a community of Christians who were anxiously awaiting the return of Jesus. They were living in the North African city of Corinth that had simply an atrocious reputation for its moral life in a declining Roman empire not noted for its high standards of human behavior. Prostitutes in many sections of the empire were often referred to as Corinthian girls. In other words, if other Romans thought that Corinth was a bad place, it must have been really bad.

One does not have to be a dualist to recognize that passions and appetites can cause one to act in life-destroying ways. This Christian community was living in the midst of moral chaos. Paul had enough insight into human nature to realize that the community of believers would not go unaffected by the larger society. He appreciated the difficulty that the Christians in this community had in living a life of responsible commitment.

Paul was not a modern person whose environment encouraged him to appreciate the positive qualities of passions, appetites, and emotions. He lived in a society that was struggling for a basic order and sense of human respect. His view of marriage as a way for the Corinthians to control their urges is understandable then if seen in this light. However, for those who go to the New Testament without any background and are simply looking for inspiration for daily life, the message of 1 Corinthians 7 is indeed difficult.

There are a number of reasons why Paul's counsel strikes a strange chord with the modern Christian. The crux of the problem, however, can be seen in verse 5. The religious imagery of this passage sees daily life as a distraction from God. Those involved with the cares of a spouse or of children are taken from concentrating solely and completely on God. Today, by contrast, most see the search for God and daily life as being harmonious. One contributes to the other. They are not at odds.

Paul advises the married couple not to separate unless "by mutual consent for a time, to devote yourselves to prayer." In other words the relationship between the spouses is seen as a hindrance in their attempt to reach God. This tension is made clear by other passages not quoted in the opening verses. For example, verses 32–33 of the same chapter explicitly state:

> I should like you to be free of all worries. The unmarried man is busy with the Lord's affairs, concerned with pleasing the Lord; but the married man is busy with this world's demands and occupied with pleasing his wife. This means he is divided.

The following diagram captures the way Paul presents the husband and wife relationship as it interferes with the search for God. The spouses who wish to find God can do so most effectively as they separate from each other and look for God in their private or communal prayer. The benefits of withdrawing from the domestic life of the family is clearly stated. The spouses can find God better if they can escape from the demands of daily life, because there is no direct connection between household chores and the search for God. With time so short, the individual would be well advised to do the work of the Lord.

By contrast to the above way of thinking, most modern Christians are more comfortable seeing daily life and the search for the holy on a continuum. One discovers God in the true depths of the other, the true depths of the self, or the true depths of creation. In other words, this is God's creation, and God is the ground of all that exists. True, one can be distracted by the pursuit of material goods. True, one can be corrupted by misusing the goods and people of this world. True, one can frantically pursue the self and its needs and land in a wallow of aimlessness and isolation. However, if one probes the mystery of the world and others by treating them with respect and reverence, then one finds the sacred that lies at the mysterious depths of everything.

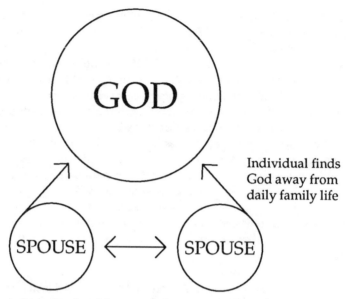

Individual finds
God away from
daily family life

Spouses should separate from each other to allow time
with God.

Put in these terms, the marriage relationship is often seen today as a
way of discovering God and not a hindrance in one's journey to God.
There is no need to withdraw from the daily chores and rhythms of life.
God is found at the heart of all creation. Everything, especially a loving
spouse, can be the source of discovering God. The diagram below would
capture how this way of thinking sees the relationship of marriage and
the search for God.

The contrast between the two mentalities, then, is telling. Paul presents his Christian ideal in the final sentence of the passage quoted. He
tells his readers, "Given my preference, I should like you to be as I am."

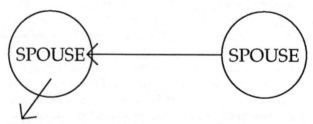

God found in the true depths of daily life, especially in
the true depths of a loved one.

What did Paul mean by this challenge? Obviously he was calling those who could hear his message to the celibate life. In all probability he was married at one time. After he became a Christian, his wife either died, left him because of his conversion, or he left her because she would not live in peace with his Christian calling. His present vocation, however, was to remain unmarried. He gave his complete effort to serving the Lord. He worked tirelessly in spreading the word and was intent on supporting himself in his own trade so that he would not be a burden on any of the local communities.

Paul finishes the chapter by exhorting his listeners on items that are consistent with his opening verses. He encourages both widows and virgins to remain unmarried if possible. He is clear that they commit no wrong if they decide to marry. By grouping virgins and widows together, he clearly shows that he is not working within the dynamics of a dualistic worldview. Sexuality is not the issue. The cares of this world, even the self-sacrificing of the mother caring for her children, are simply distracting in the search for God.

His advice to those already married is to remain together. They have made a commitment and should honor it. He does admit that those who converted after their marriage may face particularly difficult situations. Often the spouse may not have any respect for the Christian calling. Still, Paul urges the Christian to remain with the unbeliever if possible. The one who has found the faith may be the source of conversion for the spouse. If everything fails in an attempt to win peace with the unbelieving spouse and he or she wishes to leave, then one should let such a spouse go.

Paul's treatment of marriage in his letter to the Corinthians is the most direct and forceful statement of the theology of marriage in the New Testament. But it cannot be understood without Ephesians 5. The two passages balance each other and foreshadow the constant struggle the tradition will have in giving marriage its due while still accounting for how overwhelming the personal call of God can be.

God's activity in marriage captures the heart of the redemptive initiative in the world. Still, Christians who experience the intensity of a personal calling from God have a difficult time focusing on the concerns of daily family living.

Some of the passages in the Corinthian text reflect the peculiar quirks Paul faced in dealing with a Christian community known for its radical behavior in a city that had its own struggles with chaos. However, the main thrust of the passage urges Christians to put the preparation for the kingdom above everything else. While not the final or complete word of the New Testament, this message does capture the main thrust of the early Christian teaching. The Christians were a people who were obsessed with the expected coming of Jesus to establish a new order.

The theology of marriage is in fact never treated in an extended way outside the epistles. It simply was not central to the concerns of the earliest Christians. They were taken with preparing for the kingdom. They presumed the message spelled out in Paul's letter.

Marriage and family, of course, could not be ignored in the other books of the New Testament. To the first century Jews who were the original audience of Jesus and who were for the most part the intended audience for the New Testament, family was as central as the study of the Old Testament would suggest. If Jesus were to be an effective teacher, therefore, he would have to draw heavily upon the family images that were so dear to the hearts of his listeners.

B. The Family Image in the New Testament

Family images are certainly used in the New Testament. The images were used, however, to teach a lesson about the central theme that runs throughout the New Testament—prepare for the kingdom for it will come in its fullness shortly.

Each treatment of the family usually brings out a slightly different message. Each however is clearly related to the kingdom.

The Family of Jesus

Combing the volumes of pious literature today, the reader can uncover long treatises on the domestic life of the holy family. Volumes have been written about Joseph. Dramas have been developed about the domestic skills of Mary. The fact is, however, that the New Testament was not interested in the domestic virtues found in the common life of Jesus, Mary, and Joseph. It was intent on simply keeping the focus on the kingdom.

The gospel accounts did not address whether Joseph was a good carpenter or not. They did not mention whether he taught Jesus how to make doorstops. They did not even concern themselves with how Mary and Joseph got along in daily life. On the contrary, whenever the family of Jesus is mentioned, the writers of the gospels simply used the incident to teach about the kingdom.

We know virtually nothing about Joseph except that he was fairly kind to Mary. When he found her with child, he was going to put her away quietly rather than hold her up to public punishment. However, that point is incidental to the main lesson. Joseph was at the complete disposal of God's will. The gospel writers wanted to drive home the central message that Joseph lived to do the will of God. They wanted to show this obedience as the governing principle of his life.

When he finds that Mary is with child by God's design, he takes her as his wife. When he receives instruction that the family is in danger, he immediately obeys God and removes the family to Egypt. When instruction comes that it is safe to return to Palestine, Joseph picks up and returns to his homeland.

Whatever the facts of the situation may have been, it is obvious that the gospel writers are crafting a lesson for their readers. They continually insist that those who wish to enter the kingdom must be like Joseph. They must do the will of God. They must exist to do the will of God.

Similarly, the message is basically the same with the treatment of Mary. She is mentioned a little more frequently than Joseph. The point made time after time, however, can be summarized in the canticle assigned her when she learns that she has been chosen the mother of God. The passage reads:

> My being proclaims the greatness of the Lord,
>   my spirit finds joy in God my savior,
> For he has looked upon his servant in her lowliness;
>   all ages to come shall call me blessed.
> God who is mighty has done great things for me,
>   holy is his name. . . .
>   (Lk 1:46–49)

As with Joseph, the main point is that Mary's person, her life, her being, honors God. She calls others to an awareness of God by her willingness to do anything that pleases God or that forwards his designs for the world. This is what the disciples of Jesus must strive to achieve in their personal lives if they want to enter the kingdom.

The message of the gospel writers was persistent. It did not slacken even when treating the interaction of the son and parents. In the one scene mentioned where Jesus and both his parents deal directly with each other, there is little domestic tranquility. Jesus is returning from a visit to the temple with his parents. After a day's travel they discover that he is missing. They return to Jerusalem in search of him.

When they find Jesus in the temple on the third day after he was missing, he is mildly reprimanded by his mother, "Son, why have you done this to us? You see that your father and I have been searching for you in sorrow" (Lk 2:48). In response, Jesus does not say that he is sorry that his parents worried so much. The gospel accounts present him as oblivious to the worry and concern of his parents. In fact he replies, "Why did you search for me? Did you not know I had to be in my Father's house?" (Lk 2:49).

In many ways the scene is insensitive to any of the domestic concerns one might try to bring forth. Readers sometimes react to the report that it took Joseph and Mary a full day to realize that Jesus was missing. However, what the story implies is probably a rather fluid extended family unit that traveled together. More to the point, however, the gospel writers blunt any interchange between a loving son and his concerned parents. The family reactions are short-circuited by the assertion that God's work takes precedence over anything. The parents of Jesus should recognize this reality. The problem is theirs.

Put in easier terms, the gospel writers were trying to assert that domestic life must give way for the kingdom and its preparation. There simply was no interest in the virtues of home life. Were it not for the expectations of the impending events—what is called in the tradition the eschatological expectations—the gospel writers no doubt would have given more attention to the family setting. Indeed, when the second coming did not materialize, the Christian community was flooded with apocryphal literature which included among its major themes the domestic life of the family of Jesus. In other words, many writings appeared and tried to pass themselves off as written in the time of Jesus or at least taken from sources that originated during the time of Jesus. These writings clearly show how the hunger for domestic details rushes to the forefront with the retreat of the eschatological expectations.

Finally, there is one more scene which perhaps rounds out the treatment of the domestic life of Jesus. In the second chapter of John's gospel he reports that Jesus and his mother attended a wedding feast together. Nothing is said of Joseph. As might be expected in accounts which give such little stock to the domestic setting, if Joseph had died by the time Jesus reached his public life in his late twenties, the gospels did not see fit to report it.

The scene at Cana is meant to depict the dramatic way that Jesus proclaims his mission to the world. He performs his first public miracle. He does it at the request of his mother before he is prepared to give public witness. His time had not yet come.

St. John's gospel has a number of different ways of trying to emphasize the importance of Mary. This is one of them. But even given his desire to place Mary into a position of prominence, John does not dwell on a warm interchange of feeling between mother and son. The mother simply informs the son that the hosts have run out of wine. The son replies, "Woman, how does this concern of yours involve me? My hour has not yet come" (Jn 2:4). The mother responds by simply telling the servants: "Do whatever he tells you" (Jn 2:5).

Obviously, John is attempting to honor the mother. But even granted that the term "woman" was one of honor in its day, the writer was obviously not interested in honoring her in her capacity of domestic mother. Family is once again pushed aside, and Mary is honored in some formal way as she initiates the work of the kingdom.

Readers who approach the New Testament, then, must realize that its books are designed around a central message for a given audience. The message was not that family life is the way to God. The message proclaimed quite loudly that everything of this world, including the family, must be put aside. They are but of passing importance.

The Prodigal Son

A slightly different message about the kingdom is developed in the story of the prodigal son. Where the treatment of Mary and Joseph taught what qualities were necessary to enter the kingdom, this parable drives home the point that it is never too late to prepare for the kingdom no matter what type of life one has led. No matter how bad one has been, no matter how serious the offense, all will be forgiven by God the loving Father.

The use of the family in this passage is significant in many ways. First, the image of God is that of a loving Father. This is the dominant image of God throughout the New Testament. It shows that the experience of a loving father made sense to the experience of the people in that day. Perhaps the family was not primarily a unit of intimacy as it is today. Certainly, though, the experience of a loving family must have been common enough to the first century Jews; otherwise, the image of a loving father would not make sense.

Second, the choice of sin is significant. Nothing could be harder for the people of the time to understand than a father who would give of the family's property to a son who wanted to go on his own. To divide the property before the death of the father was almost an unthinkable act of love given the values of the day. Even more incomprehensible was a son who would be so unappreciative as to waste these precious goods in loose, irresponsible living.

To bring the tale one step further and picture a father who would open his arms in welcome to such a son would definitely challenge the imagination of Jesus' audience. If this is the way God would act, then truly it is never too late to repent no matter what the hour, no matter what the fault.

Rejecting the Family

To some extent, the story of the prodigal son may not be as shocking today as it was to the audience of Jesus. We have many examples of indulging our children. We also have many examples of ungrateful children. Many readers can, then, resonate with the story of the prodigal son. Few on the other hand can easily work with the passages in which Jesus apparently challenges family loyalties and ties.

At the end of one of his teaching sessions, Jesus is informed: "Your mother and brothers and sisters are outside asking for you." His response is fairly abrupt: "Who are my mother and my brothers?" Looking around at his audience he concludes, "Whoever does the will of God is brother and sister and mother to me" (Mk 3:32–35).

This challenge dismisses what was of first importance for these people. Their lives revolved around their families. Jesus is proclaiming that God and the fellowship that existed among those who lived in the spirit of God took precedence over the family.

It was indeed a hard saying, but there is a harder saying yet. Luke's gospel has its own challenge to the family in which Jesus proclaims, "If anyone comes to me without turning his back on his father and mother, his wife and children, his brothers and sisters, indeed his very self, he cannot be my follower" (Lk 14:26).

Frequently, Jesus challenged his audience in a jolting way. This is obviously what is being done in these passages. Was it the intention of either passage to attack the family? No, in the sense that family was not the issue. Rather, the intent was to emphasize that the work of God must take precedence over everything in life including something as important as family.

Actually there are two points to such passages. There is the ideal presented to these people that God must be the center of their lives. There is also the very practical challenge. Many of the early Christians embraced the faith only after direct opposition from their families. They in fact had to be ready to renounce their family if they wished to embrace the message of Jesus.

Anyone who is converted to a radical religious calling often comes into conflict with other members of the family who are intensely religious in a different way, are only casually religious, or are not religious at all. The values and concerns that govern the converted member of the family are significantly different from those which guide other members. Such differences do not have to lead to a break in the family, but where there are significant differences, there can be pronounced tensions if not a break-up of the family.

In cases where the religion is counter-cultural, there is almost sure to be a rift in the family. The convert is drawn to a value system that radically challenges the norms governing the lives of other members of the family. In our own culture one can simply appreciate the difficulties families have with their members who join the Moonies or the Hare Krishnas. Putting aside their methods of conversion, these religions challenge in a fundamental way many of the presuppositions that serve as the fabric of a given family's lifestyle.

The Martha and Mary Story

The radical character of Jesus' call is developed in perhaps a gentler way in the account in which he visits the house of Martha. While the message is presented in a gentler fashion, it is no less persistent.

During his travels, Jesus stops at the house of a woman called Martha. He begins to teach. Eventually he is confronted by the owner who is busy caring for the needs of the guests. She insists that her sister Mary, who has been listening to the teachings of Jesus, should help her with the chores so necessary to please such a large gathering. She wants Jesus to reprimand her sister.

Jesus' response to the complaint is direct: "Martha, Martha, you are anxious and upset about many things. One thing only is required" (Lk 10:38–41).

To those familiar with the context of the saying, the "one thing" is very obvious. Nothing should take precedence over the preparation for the kingdom of God. Mary was listening to the teachings about the kingdom. This was far more important than the domestic concerns of the household which were absorbing Martha.

The message of the text is consistent with the previous ones. It is interesting from a number of different angles. First, we learn that Martha welcomed Jesus to "her home." A woman's position obviously had improved over the days of the Old Testament. Second, the passage is indicative of the unique treatment of women in Jesus' ministry. Women were allowed to travel with Jesus' entourage and listen to his message. This was indeed unusual in the first century Jewish religious setting.

Most scholars argue that Jesus' treatment of women shows that he made a concentrated attempt to uplift their position. And in fact during the early years of the community there is evidence of women taking unique positions of leadership. (For further study of this issue the reader is referred to the suggested readings at the end of the chapter.) What is important for the present concern of family life is what this challenge to the male-dominated culture must have meant for the family life of the first Christians. It must have presented some challenge to them in the daily flow of the husband and wife relationship.

In the long run the challenge seemed to be more than the community was able to meet. The patriarchal lifestyle was so deeply ingrained in the fabric of the culture that the male dominance was almost bound to rise to the surface. In fact one can see the struggle in the New Testament itself. The earlier passages seem to resonate with the improved position of women. The later writings, composed in the last decade of the first century or later, by contrast present positions on women that seem almost irreconcilable with the original teachings of Jesus. Thus, in 1 Timothy 2:12–15 one finds the following passage:

> I do not permit a woman to act as a teacher, or in any way to have authority over a man; she must be quiet. For Adam was created first, Eve afterward; moreover, it was not Adam who was deceived but the woman. It was she who was led astray and fell into sin. She will be saved through childbearing, provided she continues in faith and love and holiness—her chastity, of course, being taken for granted.

Again, the woman question is not the central concern to the present text. What is of present concern is what the New Testament writings suggest about the fabric of family life among the early Christians. The struggles must have been difficult. One can get some hint of the dilemma that the early Christians faced when one examines the vacillation of St. Paul on this question.

In passages such as 1 Corinthians 11:8–10, Colossians 3:18, and Ephesians 5:22–24, there is a general submission of women to men. The Corinthian text maintains: "A man, on the other hand, ought not to cover his head, because he is the image of God and the reflection of his glory. Woman, in turn, is the reflection of his glory." In Ephesians wives are told to "be submissive to their husbands." The letter goes on to compare the marriage bond to the bond between Christ and the church. The comparison parallels Christ to the husband and the wife to the church.

Looking at these passages, then, one could easily conclude that Paul had no doubt about the status of women. They were to be in a secondary position to men in all things. Whether one is addressing the church or the domestic scene, women are subject to men. But that is not the whole of Paul. Even where the language is one of inequality, the passages stress the deep reverence and respect that should exist between the spouses. Paul offers little doubt as to the call that the husband has to honor, love, and respect his wife as he would respect himself or as he would have Christ respect members of the church.

Paul goes even further, though, in his positioning of women. There is a part of Paul that simply wants to challenge any inequality. In 1 Corinthians 11:11–12 one finds Paul saying, "Yet, in the Lord, woman is not independent of man, nor man independent of woman. In the same way that woman was made from man, so man is born of woman; and all is from God." One also finds Paul stating in Galatians 3:27–28 the following:

> All of you who have been baptized into Christ have clothed yourselves with him. There does not exist among you Jew or Greeks, slave or freeman, male or female. All are one in Christ Jesus.

There seems to be a real struggle in Paul. Facing the call of radical unity and love in the Lord, all distinctions seem to evaporate. Faced with the practical decisions of daily life as he tries to advise the communities struggling with the thorny issues of their lives, he falls back into the prejudices of his culture.

In all probability this tension existed in the lives of the earliest Christian families as they struggled with the message of Jesus which called all to be brothers and sisters in Christ. All the evidence seems to indicate that for the most part, the male prejudice won out over the Christian message in the ensuing centuries. Many of the statements about women by the early leaders of the church, the fathers of the church, would clearly shock the modern audience.

C. The New Testament Teaching on Divorce

The only time that the gospels address the nature of marriage is when Jesus is responding to a question about divorce. When confronted by a direct question as to whether divorce was permitted, Jesus quotes the second creation account: "Have you not read that at the beginning the Creator made them male and female and declared, 'For this reason a man shall leave his father and mother and cling to his wife, and the two shall become as one'?" (Mt 19:4–5).

With that as a background, Jesus lays out a strong condemnation of divorce. The passage is similar in Matthew, Mark, and Luke which are known as the synoptic gospels because they have many passages in common, with slight adjustments to meet the peculiar needs of the intended audiences.

Mark and Luke are fairly straightforward in their condemnation of divorce. Matthew, however, does have, for many modern Christians, a troubling exception. After addressing the prohibition of divorce, Matthew has Jesus say "except for *porneia*." The term could be translated as fornication, immorality, or incest. A number of important scholars make a good case for arguing that the exception is addressing marriage within the forbidden limits of blood relationship as stated in Leviticus 18:6–18. The issue, however, cannot easily be put to rest.

If there is any doubt about how culturally shocking Jesus' message was to his audience, Matthew leaves little doubt. His disciples state in disbelief, "If that is the case between man and wife, it is better not to marry" (Mt 19:10). Jesus simply responds, "Let him accept this teaching who can" (Mt 19:12).

Other passages dealing with divorce can be found in the fifth chapter of Matthew, the tenth chapter of Mark, the sixteenth chapter of Luke, and in Paul's letter to the Corinthians. They do not add anything very different to Matthew's treatment except to acknowledge the possibility of the woman also divorcing the man. In condemning that practice as well, these passages were probably reflecting their audiences who were dispersed throughout the Roman empire and were familiar with the Roman law allowing women to divorce their husbands, a practice unknown to Jewish law.

The New Testament writers clearly showed that they were rejecting the ways of the Old Testament. They have the Pharisees challenging Jesus by arguing that Moses allowed divorce in the Old Testament. Jesus counters by charging that Moses permitted this simply because of the hardness of their hearts. He knew, in other words, that the Israelites could not live up to the ideal. Jesus, though, insists that to be his follower one must live up to the ideal set forth in the creation account.

D. The New Testament Teachings About Children

Needless to say, with such a limited emphasis on the family, there is very limited attention given to children in any of the books of the New Testament. Despite the many pious paintings and pictures depicting Jesus taken with angelic young ones, the writers of the early Christian literature were not drawn to focus on children.

One passage that stands out despite its brevity is a scene in which Jesus blesses the children who are brought to him. The disciples who see the people pressing upon Jesus rebuke the people to leave the Lord alone. Jesus will have none of it, however. He responds, "Let the little children come to me. Do not shut them off" (Lk 18:16). The next verse puts the incident into perspective. Jesus continues to state, "The reign of God belongs to such as these" (Lk 18:16).

Just as all the other domestic passages were designed to teach a lesson about preparing for the kingdom, this passage is no exception. Those who wish to participate in the new order must realize that "whoever does not accept the kingdom of God as a child will not enter into it" (Lk 18:17).

The passage is interesting for the way children are offered as the norm for behavior. In a sense Jesus reverses the normal roles. Children for the most part were considered imperfect adults. Evidence does not suggest they were placed in any special privileged position as in many sectors of our culture. Nevertheless, Jesus offers the simple, trusting faith of the child as the norm for his disciples.

There are not any other substantial texts dealing with children aside from the few domestic counsels offered in the letters to local communities. In Colossians 3:18 and Ephesians 6:1–4, for example, we find essentially the same message. Children are urged to honor and obey their parents. Certainly this is a message that fits in well with the Jewish family customs of the day. He also goes on in both passages to warn the father not to be harsh with the children lest they lose heart. Paul urges his fellow Christians to instruct their children in the spirit of the Lord.

Such a loving counsel is interesting in view of some of the harsher Christian attitudes toward raising children that will develop in succeeding centuries. When Christianity becomes immersed in a sense of original sin, a dualistic worldview, and a hierarchical society, its main caution is often the need to break the rebellious will of the child.

CONCLUSION

The ideal of New Testament community is pictured in the passage from the Acts of the Apostles in which the early Christians are depicted as living in a community where goods were freely shared according to the legitimate needs of each member. The passage reads:

> They devoted themselves to the apostles' instruction and the communal life, to the breaking of bread and the prayers. A reverent fear overtook them all, for many wonders and signs were performed by the apostles. Those who believed shared all things in common; they would

sell their property and goods, dividing everything on the basis of each one's need. They went to the temple area together every day, while in their homes they broke bread. With exultant and sincere hearts they took their meals in common, praising God and winning the approval of all the people (Acts 2:42–47).

The ideal for the Old Testament can be captured to some extent in Psalms 127 and 128. The first reads in part:

Behold sons are a gift from the Lord; the fruit of the womb is a reward.
Like arrows in the hand of a warrior are the sons of one's youth.
Happy the man whose quiver is filled with them. . . .
(Ps 127:3–5)

The second psalm reads in part:

Your wife shall be like a fruitful vine in the recesses of your home;
Your children like olive plants around your table.
Behold, thus is the man blessed who fears the Lord.
(Ps 128:3–4)

The question these quite different views of life offer to the Christian of the present time is challenging. If scripture is to be taken as a norm, what does it possibly have to say to someone seeking guidance for family life today? Indeed the domestic life is so culturally conditioned that every Christian community at different points in history does in fact present its own peculiar versions of family. There are even radical shifts within relatively short time periods. No change could be more dramatic than what was witnessed within the scriptures themselves.

The reality is that scripture is not a handbook of family living. It is a challenging journey by a people who reflect on their experience of God, the Jesus event. What these people have to say to succeeding generations is not easily translated. It requires one to listen carefully to the message. David Tracy suggests the best way to appreciate the challenge of scripture is to accept it as the religious classic for the Christian community.[1]

A classic delves so deeply and intensely into the fabric of life in a given period that it has a universal significance. It captures something that is so basic to the life of an age that the underlying reality is a ground found in the life of any age. Applied to the Christian scriptures, the writings of the Old and the New Testaments capture in such a fundamental way the experience and meaning of God in human life that every age must listen to the witness of these people.

Obviously, the translation for something as peculiar as family life will not be easy. For the sake of the present study, certain points will be articulated as hopefully helpful in appreciating the New Testament challenge. No simple list of a few points is adequate, of course. Nevertheless, they may stimulate discussion.

What must be avoided is a triumphant Christianity. Christianity does not simply challenge, it learns from the insights of each culture. It should expect to learn from these cultures. Human societies are formed in response to the movements of creation, a creation that is grounded in God.

The first key point by which later Christian communities must be measured is whether they adequately appreciate the special value of each individual. Both testaments insist that each person has a unique relationship with God. If God cares so much as to continually pursue and forgive his people they must be something of great worth.

Following that position, Christians should insist on the depth of mystery contained in each marital relationship. Where two people who are special to God promise a lifelong relationship, there can be no trivial promises. There must be a bonding that reaches to the depths of the couple's life.

Paradoxically, a third point that the scriptures insist upon is that people are going to fail. Furthermore, they are going to fail in significant ways. All the main characters of the Old Testament have major failures —Abraham, Sarah, Isaac, Rebecca, Jacob, Moses, David. All the disciples of Christ likewise have their embarrassing failures—Peter, James, John, Thomas. There were not simply dramatic failures. Frequently there were petty failures such as the mother of James and John urging that her sons be placed at the right hand of Jesus.

Such a view clearly challenges the prevalent sense of romantic love. The couple might walk off into the sunset. The sun, however, moves faster than anyone can walk. Soon darkness will fall. Hopefully the light of day will be equally present as the relationship continues. There will be dark moments.

A fourth challenge that the scriptures offer future generations of Christians is that they sense the call to pass on life. The world is seen as a place of importance and meaning. Humans are seen as having a pivotal role in bringing that destiny or meaning to fruition. This contribution to life is certainly not limited to making babies. There is an awareness that discipleship, parenthood, or mentorship is a challenge that taxes the full range of one's talents. Contributing to new physical life is but one way of giving to the reaching for life. In marriage, however, children would naturally be a primary way of passing on life to future generations.

These then will be the four points that will continually emerge in the Christian response to a given culture. Others may likewise emerge given the peculiar quirks of a particular culture. These, however, will be recurrent themes.

NOTE

1. David Tracy, "The Particularity and Universality of Christian Revelation," *Revelation and Experience* (New York: Seabury Press, 1979) p. 112.

STUDY QUESTIONS

1. What one event dominates the New Testament attitude toward daily life?

2. What is the basic message of Ephesians 5?

3. What is the purpose of marriage in 1 Corinthians 7:1–6?

4. Discuss the tension between these two texts.

5. Contrast how Paul counsels the married couple searching for God with how modern Christians see the married life and the quest for God.

6. How was the family used in the New Testament teachings?

7. What is the New Testament teaching on divorce?

FURTHER STUDY

Martin, Thomas M. *Christian Family Values* (New York: Paulist Press, 1984). A readable book that devotes two chapters to the family in scripture.

Ruether, Rosemary Radford, ed. *Religion and Sexism* (New York: Simon and Schuster, 1974). Excellent essays on how religion has treated women with some giving particular attention to women in scripture.

Schillebeeckx, Edward. *Marriage* (New York: Sheed and Ward, 1965). Excellent for developing the theology of marriage in scripture.

Theissen, Gerd. *The Social Setting of Pauline Christianity* (Philadelphia: Fortress Press, 1982). Shows how family served the early Christian community.

Travard, George. *Women in Christian Tradition* (Notre Dame: University of Notre Dame Press, 1973). Amid the broader treatment, there is attention given to women in scripture.

4.

Marriage in the Patristic Period

——————— ◇ ———————

The second century slave, the twentieth century nuclear physicist, the eighth century emperor, the twentieth century slum dweller in Haiti, the sixteenth century convert in China—all embrace the Christian faith. In their profession of faith, however, they bring a personal history, a cultural experience which influences how they compose the Christian story for their own personal journey.

Any abrupt change of culture is disorienting. This past summer a group of university students went to China to study. Their instructor was a young man who grew up in the country but had not been back there for three years. Their trip was not a typical tourist excursion. Rather, they stayed in the dormitories of a local university and went economy all the way. They experienced the diet, the hygiene, the social decorum, the toilet practices, the travel hardships, and the economic toil of the average resident in a way that escapes the typical tourist. The result was culture shock.

One student could not sleep. She could not eat. She could not socialize even with her American classmates. She spent considerable time staring into space. By contrast, her instructor came alive. His juices flowed with the excitement of eating these traditional dishes and living in surroundings so familiar to his childhood. Obviously, for him the experience was not weighed on some objective scale of nutrition and cleanliness. No, he was touching base with his roots, his fundamentals. He quickly snuggled into a comfortable way of life that was home for him.

The way people react when they are moved from one setting to another gives some clue as to how the cultural setting of believers colors every aspect of their faith. In turn, the individual faith of the community members moves the community in a distinct direction. The culture and the faith tradition dialogue. Neither leaves the other untouched.

In an attempt to show how the church struggled to put marriage and family into perspective throughout the ages, this chapter will look at the period immediately after the New Testament—the patristic period. Subsequent chapters will show the adjustments made in the medieval period, the reformation period, and the modern period. Such a sampling of how the tradition interacted with different points in cultural development will also help the community understand how it must challenge the present structure of human life while at the same time learning from it.

The period after the New Testament is generally called the patristic period or the period of the fathers. It runs roughly from the second century to the eighth century. It receives its name from the formative influence that many of the early leaders of the church had in setting the tone for future Christianity. These influential leaders were almost exclusively men. Such a pattern would be expected given the culture of the day. Such a pattern also placed limitations on Christian awareness because its self-understanding was so dominated by male celibates.

The New Testament period covers the greater part of the first century of the present era. During the closing decades of that century the Christian community faced a very difficult decision. When the second coming did not take place, Christianity had to ask whether it was meant for all peoples or whether it was simply to be a reform movement within Judaism. It is a fact that throughout most of the first century the followers of Jesus were found mainly in Jewish communities spread throughout the Roman empire.

The experience of the Spirit for these early Christians, however, was so intense that they felt compelled to share their faith with all peoples. The decision which came to a dramatic head in the Council of Jerusalem is not a surprising one. Most intense religions feel the call to share the excitement of their faith. The decision, however, was not without its complications.

In its attempt to become intelligent to the larger community, the church had to overcome a significant cultural barrier. The many peoples within the Roman empire would not be able to understand the myriad Jewish images, references, and ways of thinking that made such sense to the original disciples of Jesus.

A. Two Basic Choices

The community had two basic choices. It could try to teach prospective converts to understand the Jewish culture so that the message of Christianity would be intelligible to them. On the other hand, it could try to translate Christianity into terms that made sense to the many people spread throughout the empire. In practical terms this second option required the advocates to translate Christianity into Greek images and lifestyles.

The Romans contributed much to human society through their innovations in government organization, law, social structure, military planning, and economic initiative. However, the empire was greatly indebted to the Greeks for their way of investigating the meaning of human efforts and their ability to articulate the values that flowed from their different approaches to the destiny of human life.

The second century challenge of translating Christian beliefs from one culture to another was similar to what Christianity faced in the sixteenth century. In the 1500s, through the discoveries, explorations, and conquests by the European powers, the church established ties with the Asian countries and the Amerindians on the American continents. In the attempts to reach the people native to these regions, the church could have translated the faith into terms that made sense to the native culture. On the other hand the church could simply demand that these natives adjust to the western culture which had such a grip on the Christian way of living.

On the American continent options were not seriously considered. The conquering Europeans simply overwhelmed the native cultures. The foreigners succeeded in imposing their ways, including their religion, on the defeated. In most sections of Asia, however, the Europeans were not successful in imposing their domination. They certainly fought to establish spheres of influence. In most cases, however, they had only limited success in shaping the Asian peoples.

In countries such as China, for example, Christianity had to be prepared to speak to people in terms and images that drew from the myths and symbols of their society. Some of the early Christian missionaries such as Mateo Ricci were prepared to make these translations. However, most Christian leaders back in Europe simply received their efforts with horror and insisted that the expressions of faith must remain pure. To someone three centuries later who has the benefit of historical perspective, it is obvious that these church leaders were often prompted by cultural blindness. The sixteenth century leaders did not have the benefit of historical perspective, of course.

To some extent the question of blame is not the issue. What is important is that in fact Christianity made few adaptations to the eastern cultures. It remained basically a western religion, and, as a result, Christianity had a limited impact throughout Asia. There are a few exceptions such as in the Philippines where Christianity did prosper. This local spread of Christianity, however, usually took place in countries where the native culture was weak or fragmented.

If the early missionaries who sought to translate Christianity into the native cultures had succeeded, Christianity would in fact have been changed. Any religion that translates into a new culture undergoes a jarring evaluation. The change does not have to mean that the community is unfaithful to the originating revelation. The change is often significant enough, however, to cause many of the followers to lose their breath.

The difference between the sixteenth century and the second century Christians to some extent boiled down to a matter of choice. The earlier church simply did not have much of an alternative. It had to translate its beliefs into the images of the larger culture if it hoped to have any significant influence. Judaism was such an infinitely small subculture that it would go unnoticed by the larger empire.

Put in these terms, of course, the process of acculturation sounds very conscious and deliberate. What must be realized, however, is that the Christians were only partially aware of the fact that they were changing. Culture is subtle and pervasive. It serves as the context for human understanding and action. Most people are intent on immediate actions and goals and have little awareness of the context until the context has shifted significantly. Most of us are not aware of breathing until the air has changed significantly and the normal breathing process is threatened.

As the first and second century Christians tried to express themselves to the strange mixture of peoples and cultures that made up the Roman empire, they naturally adjusted their message. The change was gradual and subtle. It was also undeniable and irreversible. One simply has to look at the following excerpt from the First Epistle of Clement, written toward the end of the first century, to appreciate how quickly Christianity adjusted to the thinking of the times:

> There was a time when everyone who lived among you thought highly of the full virtue and firmness of your faith, admired the sweet reasonableness of your Christian piety, heralded abroad your reputation for unbounded hospitality. . . . You did all things without respect of persons and walked in accordance with the commands of God—subject to those in office and properly respectful to the presbyters of your community. You educated the minds of your young men to moderation and modesty. You exhorted girls to do their duty with a blameless, modest and pure conscience. And you taught married women to love their husbands as they should, to be subject to them according to the rule of obedience, and to manage their homes with piety and much wisdom.[1]

The first thing that strikes the reader of the above paragraph is that much of the visionary excitement so characteristic of the New Testament passages is absent. The religion of this passage makes many adjustments to the demands of daily life. This Christianity is not burning for the end times when a new order will be established. No longer are the virtues of common life dismissed—at least not entirely. Christians still felt some of the call to live beyond the cares of this world. They did have to make their adjustments however.

Several phrases jump out to show the change present:

(a) The First Epistle of Clement speaks of the "sweet reasonableness of your Christian piety." It also reports that the Christians "educated the minds of . . . young men to moderation. . . ." These virtues of reasonableness and moderation stand in stark contrast to the exhortations of the gospels.

What happened to the gospel call for radical choice in the passage, "How I wish you were one or the other—hot or cold! But because you are lukewarm, neither hot nor cold, I will spew you out of my mouth!" (Rev 3:15–16)? The gospels were intent on calling their readers to an uncompromising following of Jesus. They saw the call to discipleship challenging the very virtues of reasonableness and moderation. The gospel readers were told: "If anyone comes to me without turning his back on his father and mother, his wife and children, his brothers and sisters, indeed his very self, he cannot be my follower" (Lk 14:26). The gospels did not preach a balance and an order. They were not interested in the "sweet reasonableness" of a disciple's life.

The passage from Clement shows the adaptation of some Christians to the sense of reason and balance that would be expected from a domesticated religion. It also reflects the way Christianity drew upon many of the groups prevalent in the empire at that time, particularly the Stoics.

(b) Nothing is more indicative of how Christianity adjusted than the passages celebrating the Christian "reputation for unbounded hospitality." Put against the Martha and Mary story (Lk 10:38–41) the contrast is telling. Martha complains about Mary not helping with the chores of hospitality. Jesus reprimands the hostess and insists that Martha is busy about many things but only one is important—hearing the teachings of Jesus—and Mary will not be denied.

What a community celebrates tells much about where it is directed. The intensity of the vision for the New Testament Christians filled them with an impatience with the ordinary in life. By the end of the first century the Christians had to come to terms with the realities of daily life and had to find an expression of their Christianity within the domestic setting.

(c) The phrase "subject to those in office and properly respectful" shows how the institutional church had already begun to assert itself. The order necessary for carrying out the demands of conventional life required a certain cohesion. The type of cohesion most readily understood at the close of the first century in a patriarchal society was obedience to the males who were in charge of the community. In a more democratic day, the virtues celebrated would have been different. In the gospels the emphasis was on a more immediate relationship with the word of God or with the discipleship of Jesus. There was not an emphasis on obedience to the community leaders.

The point is not that the change is surprising. The point is not that the change is a corruption of the original message. The point is that one must expect changes such as these to take place as the Christian community finds itself in different circumstances. This inherent need for change must be understood in any attempt to grasp the shifts that have taken place in Christian thinking about marriage. The changes in the community's attitudes toward marriage did not take place in a vacuum. They are part of more fundamental changes in the life of the larger society.

B. Adjusting the Intensity

The First Epistle of Clement represents a clear example of how at least part of the Christian community toward the end of the first century made ready adjustments to the daily life around them. But not all of the community could accept the domestic call.

Many of these early Christians still felt the tension between the slow rhythm of daily life and the excitement of the Christian faith. Their zeal simply demanded a radical lifestyle of self-dedication. If the parousia was not to take place, if the new order was not to be established in their lifetime, then many had to seek different avenues for their sense of calling.

The community members struggled with how they could give their lives solely to the service of God even if the second coming was not imminent. It is important to understand how this early community wrestled with the change. Their resolution sets the context for the church's view of marriage during the first few centuries after the New Testament.

When the community had finally made some inroads into the Roman world, it looked around at the larger society in an attempt to understand itself. It faced a rather chaotic civilization caught in a desperate struggle for stability. The Christians found little attraction in the many movements of the day that promoted a reckless abandonment to the senses. Even the more modest urgings toward physical enjoyment as a way to happiness would rub rather raw against the ideal call of the New Testament.

There is something about struggle and discipline that go hand in hand with a sense of accomplishment, and the Christians wanted to have union with God. They did not see such a union as an easy achievement. The result, then, was that Christianity aligned itself with those who questioned the pleasures of the senses as being dangerous to the spirit. The times were unstable, even chaotic, and the passions and appetites were seen as running amuck. Early in its history and for understandable reasons, Christianity became locked in a dualism which saw the spirit and the body at odds.

The Stoics, the Gnostics, the Manicheans, and the Neo-Platonists were some of the groups in the first couple of centuries of the Christian era who argued that the pleasures of the world were to be either severely controlled or enthusiastically spurned. The call and the challenge such groups offered appealed to the idealism of many Christians. Each of the movements had their own pockets of influence, their own schools within the larger Christian community. At times a given group would follow the peculiarities of their school with such fervor that the Christian message was difficult to discern. The larger Christian community would exclude them in such cases.

The tendency to renounce the world and its pleasures was probably strongest in the eremitic way of life. Some Christians withdrew into the desert to embrace the life of a hermit. They practiced a life of fasting and harsh physical punishment. Sleeping, eating, sexuality, and even the comforts of friendship were renounced in an effort to place nothing between the individual Christian and the God each sought so desperately.

The hermits withdrew into the desert to deprive the senses as much as possible. Many of their practices strike the modern person as strange. Today there is a much more benign attitude toward the beauties of the world and the comforts it offers. Today people feel that life is stimulated through the senses, not distorted or misguided by them.

The church, then, developed its style of life and its reflection in this dualistic setting. Taken to its extreme, it is not difficult to understand how the eremitic lifestyle was considered the ideal of Christian living. It is also not difficult to understand how even the celibates living in the midst of the local church were honored. Like the hermit, the people of the local church who renounced the pleasures of personal intimacy were heralded as removing themselves from the lures of the present life.

C. Addressing Marriage

Given this dualism, this sense of conflict between the spirit and the body, how did the early leaders of the church address the married people in the community? In many cases it spoke to them in harsh terms. Origen, for example, who around the turn of the third century was the leader of the famous theological school at Alexandria in present day Egypt, offered the following perspective:

> How can the Apostle Paul write, "I wish the young widows to marry and beget children"? Is he commanding marriage so that bodies born of woman may furnish prisons for angels who have fallen from heaven and are turned, according to you, into souls? Or is it rather to obey God's decree about the marriage union, and to preserve the human race?[2]

The passage gives Origen's own peculiar twists to the dualism. He felt that souls pre-existed and were imprisoned in the body. The man is usually appreciated for his brilliance. He is also known for his rather eccentric positions and lifestyle. However, the main thrust of the statement captures a common theme of the fathers. Virginity is heavily favored for those who feel capable of the call. Marriage is usually presented as a concession to human weakness that allows the race to continue.

Christian thinkers at this time were quite upset with the way the married state thrust people into the midst of the physical world. So intense were their misgivings that they had a difficult time seeing marriage as part of God's plan originally. God, who wrought such wonders within creation, must have had a better way of propagating the human race. The thought of having two people thrust into the animalistic postures of intercourse seemed abhorrent for many of the early leaders. True, marriage is good because the scriptures say it is good. But to the minds of most of these early church leaders, it must have been at best a backup plan that resulted after the fall. Marriage must have been introduced after the perfect plan ran amuck with the sin of the first humans.

Marriage did have a champion of sorts. St. Augustine of Hippo, a bishop in North Africa and arguably the strongest leader of the western church during this period, did insist that marriage was a part of God's plan originally. The following passage captures his position:

> You are entirely mistaken when you think that marriage was instituted so that the passing of the dead would be compensated for by the succession of those who were born. Marriage was instituted so that the chastity of women would make sons known to their fathers and fathers to their sons.
>
> True, it was possible that men be born of promiscuous and random intercourse with any women at all, but there could not have been a bond of kinship between fathers and sons.[3]

For many this passage strikes them as strange and difficult. Augustine shows many presuppositions in this statement that are not shared by the modern reader. For example, few today would speak of births as ways of compensating for those who died. Today the fear is that there is rampant growth in the human population. For Augustine, however, everything was seen as carefully planned by God. Even the precise number of human beings was set. Prior to the fall, in the opinion of most in the early church, there was to be no death. When the predetermined number of humans was reached, there would be no more made.

However, with the introduction of death as a result of the fall, there was a need to replace human numbers with new births. The entire tone of Augustine's writings shows his passion, if one could use such a dangerous word, for order and control. He lived in a world that was coming apart at the seams. People faced with chaos readily reach for structure.

Another disturbing phrase for the modern reader should be the blatant male chauvinism in "the chastity of women would make sons known to their fathers and fathers to their sons." Again the modern reader does not have to be a feminist to appreciate that women are equal in dignity to men. Augustine's phrase almost dismisses the mother to a passive role in the life of the family. He does not even mention the daughters.

On one level this dismissal of women should shock the modern day Christian. On another level, any person familiar with history should know that women have systematically been treated as second class citizens. In fact women were often seen as imperfect males. If men struggled with concupiscence (the disharmony between appetites and the rational direction of life) women were in a far worse state as they were seen to be run by whims and feelings. They were seen as far more emotional and far less rational than men.

Despite all these barriers for the modern person, however, one should still be able to realize that Augustine sees a bond existing between parent and child that is not found in any other relationship. The family community, in other words, is seen as having special gifts that are unmatched in other human relationships. With all the depreciation of the marital union in other writings of the day, arguments such as this are important in marriage's struggle to receive proper respect.

If one reads on in Augustine, there are forceful arguments which insist that marriage was originally part of God's plan. His argument, understandably, does appear strange:

> We read that they were already expelled from paradise when they had relations and conceived children. Still I do not see what could prevent their having an honorable marriage and an immaculate marriage bed even in paradise. When they were living faithfully and justly, serving Him with obedience and holiness, God could have arranged that, without any restless ardor of sensual desire, without any labor or childbirth pain, children would be born of their seed.[4]

Once again there should be a few key phrases that show how the organizing images of life are so different for Augustine. He speaks of an "immaculate marriage bed." Augustine was simply not comfortable with the physical and the sensual. The later phrase "without any restless ardor of sensual desire" is a good clue as to what he meant by immaculate. Augustine pictured marital relations prior to the fall as being a passionless activity designed simply to achieve the very necessary end of having children by one's seed. Within the biology of the day, it was the male seed which was planted in the woman as the fertile ground. In the experience of the day, the farmer put seed in the ground to be nurtured by the earth. Similarly, the male put his seed in the woman to be nurtured by the woman's body. The realization that the woman contributes half the attributes through a fertilized egg had to await the investigations of modern medicine in the last two centuries.

Augustine goes on to explain that the reason why Adam and Eve did not have relations until after the fall was quite simple. God did not tell them to do so. Since they were not driven by unruly appetites, they had no reason to procreate. They were simply awaiting the will of God. They were waiting to be told.

The early Christian appreciation of marriage was strained then. The mainstream church, however, resisted the many forces that pushed it to speak ill of marriage. Any attempt to praise virginity by condemning the family was challenged immediately. A passage typical of those supporting marriage was issued by a local council of bishops in Gangra, Turkey in the fourth century:

> 1. If anyone disparages marriage, shuns a faithful and God-fearing wife who sleeps with her husband, and speaks as though she cannot enter the Kingdom of God, let him be anathema. . . .
>
> 9. If anyone is a virgin or celibate but is avoiding marriage because he regards it as some moral disorder and not because of virginity's own beauty and holiness, let him be anathema.
>
> 10. If anyone of those who are celibates for the Lord's sake casts aspersions on those who take wives, let him be anathema. . . .
>
> 19. If any woman deserts her husband and wishes to quit of him because she abhors marriage, let her be anathema.[5]

No matter how forceful the winds blew against marriage, scripture called marriage good. The Christian community could never ignore that reality. It is a bit like the American people and their reverence for the Declaration of Independence. This document which laid the foundation for the American spirit of government declared that all are created equal and have certain inalienable rights. Obviously there are times when the United States has not lived up to that ideal. Ask the Afro-Americans. Ask the Irish immigrants. Ask the women. The Declaration, however, put the phrase in a place where it could not be ignored. It sits there as a continual challenge to all the inequality that in fact does exist.

In a similar way, the scriptures held the church on a corrective course. Against the Gnostics, against the Manicheans, the mainstream church insisted that marriage was good. Given the presuppositions of the day, it was not easy to explain why it was good. Today, of course, the church can readily speak of how physical intimacy creates a gentle, loving relationship that nurtures the life between the partners. Such an appreciation of physical intimacy, however, presupposes that the body and the soul are complementary. Nothing could be further from the thinking of the early Christians.

D. The Good of Marriage

Where then did the early Christian community find the good of marriage? Before that question is addressed, one should realize that the agenda for the leaders of the early church was set in fairly definite terms.

They accepted the Bible literally. When they read the account of the fall, these leaders felt that they had to anchor their thought in the threefold punishment of the woman that resulted from the fall:

1. The woman was to bear her children in pain.
2. The woman was to lust after her husband.
3. The man was to be the ruler of the family.

For people who take the Bible literally, as the early leaders of the church did, the relationship between husband and wife was changed after the disobedience of Adam and Eve. The creation accounts may speak of the need for companionship and imply the complementarity of the two sexes. There was, in the minds of these early fathers of the church, a changed reality after the fall. The lust of the woman and the domination of the man moved the marriage relationship into a different order.

Because lust was seen as part of the punishment for the first sin, there was little room for celebrating the physical intimacy and companionship that a husband and wife can experience in each other. There was little room for seeing this relationship as an avenue to God. The punishment of the woman fed easily into the dualism of the day. The movements of the body were a curse and not a blessing.

In fact the bodily appetites were so suspect that marriage itself was often seen as a source of sin. Augustine, for example, would argue that any giving into venereal pleasure, the carnal pleasure of sex, is sinful. It is mortally sinful if sought outside of marriage. It is venially sinful if enjoyed within the marriage. Realizing the strength of the sexual drive, it was difficult for the early writers to imagine any act of intercourse that did not encompass some intentional enjoyment of the act. Therefore, to their way of thinking, venial sin was usually involved.

Augustine's writings are certainly influenced by his own struggle as well as by the Christian tradition. He originally belonged to the Manicheans who renounced the material world as evil. As a result he must have been overcome with feelings of guilt when he could not resist the allurements of the flesh. He kept a mistress through most of his younger years. When he finally converted from Manichean doctrines, the Christian message demanded that he take a more positive view of the world and of marriage. He did adjust. He did change. He did not, however, leave behind all his misgivings about the physical and his feelings of guilt about his earlier sexual escapades.

While Augustine, then, offers his own peculiarities, he is fairly representative of the early thinkers who had to wrestle with the dualism prevalent in their day. He is also important because he had such an influence on the thinking of the church in the centuries following.

The struggle to call marriage good was difficult for most of the early leaders of the church. But what indeed made marriage good for the community of the first couple of centuries? To phrase the question somewhat differently, what were the goods of marriage? Again, Augustine can be used to summarize the three points most frequently mentioned:

> This is threefold: fidelity, offspring, sacrament. Fidelity means that one avoids all sexual activity apart from one's marriage. Offspring means that a child is accepted in love, is nurtured in affection, is brought up in religion. Sacrament means that the marriage is not severed nor the spouse abandoned, not even so that the abandoner or the abandoned may remarry for the sake of the children.[6]

Marriage is thus seen as a way of avoiding promiscuous relationships with many people. The partners are sexually faithful to each other. This is important, of course, for many reasons. The New Testament clearly acknowledges the value of marriage in checking the drives of the passions. Sexual fidelity brings a stability to life. If the society of the day were anxious for anything, it was looking for stability in the life of its people.

The second value the church saw in marriage was the offspring it produced. There was no doubt that the work of the Lord must carry on. Marriages were needed if there were to be virgins, martyrs, and a church. Since the tradition, contrary to movements such as the Gnostics and the Manicheans, saw that God's creation was good, then the creation must continue. Marriage was the institution that kept it going.

Finally, Augustine speaks of the marriage as a sacrament. He did not use the term as it came to be developed in the medieval period. He did in fact, however, use the term in different, nuanced ways. In general, when he speaks of sacrament in marriage, he is reaching for the sense of commitment and bonding in the couple and the witness this gives to others who see the beauty of their life together.

It is not difficult to understand why the tradition would admire this commitment in the marriage. The scriptures are filled with the need for people to be faithful to their word. God is faithful to Israel. God will not abandon those who live "in the Lord." Humans must strive to be faithful to God, to their faith commitment even in the face of persecution unto death. Turning from their scriptural tradition, the Christians looked at the world around them and saw the lack of commitment as precisely the cause of so much of the chaos and disorder. With this background, there is little wonder why the church valued the fidelity it found in the life commitment among its married people.

E. The Practice of Marriage

To those born into today's Christian community where a church wedding is seen as something important, it is rather surprising to realize that the early Christians simply got married according to the civil customs and ceremonies of the day. Today where there are many rules and regulations developed in the church tradition, people have simply become accustomed to the church not only approving of the marriage but also presiding over it as official witness.

But for many centuries the church did not step into the forefront of marriage practices. It was not until the middle ages where the church and the state became closely intertwined that the church took a major role in governing marriages. On the contrary, in the earliest decades of the community, Christians considered themselves as reformers within Judaism. They continued to attend Jewish services, and scripture for them was the Hebrew Bible. It was only after several decades that they came to look upon their calling as one distinct from Judaism. It was only after their tradition jelled that they began to look upon their own literature as a New Testament.

It is not surprising, then, that the early church did not set up its own forms of the marriage ceremony or its own laws governing the practice of marriage. In fact the Synod of Elvira at the start of the fourth century clearly acknowledged that Christians observed the same ceremonies as do the non-Christians.[7]

There was, of course, pastoral concern on the part of the church. It advised its people on the qualities that were to be nurtured in marriage. At least implied in that counsel would be the type of person who would make a good Christian spouse. There are a few instances in which some of the early leaders such as Ignatius of Antioch and Tertullian counseled that the advice of the bishop should be sought prior to marriage. There is little evidence that the practice was widespread, however.

Around the fourth century there did develop a practice of the bishop or the priest blessing the married couple after the marriage. What is surprising is that the practice took so long to develop. One would think that people who centered their life around their religious community would naturally want that community to in some way or another officially acknowledge or bless that new life. Perhaps the ceremony was slow in developing because of the church's struggle with accepting the reality of marriage as part of God's original plan.

While the practice of the blessing and then the solemnization of the marriage often in connection with the eucharistic service grew, it did not become widespread for many centuries. For the first one thousand years of its history, the church did not require its members to have their marriage solemnized by its official presence or approval.

During the patristic period the church was drawn into the marriage issues only in special cases. At times the involvement was functional. If orphans were placed under the care of the bishop, he had to act the part of the parent. At times the involvement was prompted by institutional concerns. Special regulations, for example, were laid down for the marriage of the clergy. The church had to assure that its clergy led exemplary lives and would naturally feel the need to govern the marriages of its leaders.

At times the involvement was prompted by the theology of marriage prevalent in that period. For example, it frowned upon second marriages. If a widow or widower were to marry, there would be in most cases little likelihood that they could have children. Since children were the only justification for sexual relations, there were serious questions why the widowed couple would want to marry again. In general, the community expressed strong reservations about second marriages. Often it refused to extend its blessing upon the union.

Similarly, seeking to be remarried after a divorce was not generally acceptable within the community. The extensive discussion of whether or not divorce was ever permitted in the early church need not be considered here. The disagreements about the divorce question arise in terms of whether any community at any time permitted divorce. There is general consensus among scholars that generally the early church did not permit divorce and remarriage. The tradition from scripture against divorce was strong enough and the misgivings against marriage were prevalent enough that the community would not look favorably upon someone switching partners.

The early church saw the Christian calling as a demanding one. Christians considered one of the essential marks of the church to be its holiness. If a member of the community failed significantly, there was serious question about whether the offender could continue in the community. Generally, a member was allowed one reception of the sacrament of penance for a serious offense such as adultery. The penance and reconciliation were public and were extended over a year or more.

Once married, then, the couple were expected to remain faithful to each other. Any serious failure within the marriage was considered a reason for questioning the person's presence in the community.

Aside from these situations where the church was thrust into the marriage practices of its members either because of peculiar legal situations, inherent discipline questions, or theological reservations, the church also offered pastoral advice. Exhortations in sermons and in the daily prayer life of the community were to be expected.

CONCLUSION

At the end of the previous chapter, four points were laid out in an attempt to capture some of the heritage that the church took on its journey through the shifting cultures. Scripture warned that people would fail in their own personal journeys. It insisted that, despite these failures, all were precious to God. Third, it called marriage good. And, finally, marriage had a role to play in the plan of salvation.

All of these points did not translate easily into the church's attempt to enter the Roman world. Thrust into the dualism of the time, Christians had no trouble realizing that people will fail. There was little or no tendency to exaggerate the value of marriage and family life. In a sense the problem was weighted toward the negative side. Marriage and family were so steeped in the physical world, it was evident that members of any family were constantly failing.

It was only the second and third points—the scriptural insistence on the value of each individual and the scriptural declaration that marriage is good—that challenged the church leaders to appreciate marriage. They did learn to appreciate marriage for the love and commitment that developed between the spouses and between the parents and the siblings. They did appreciate the witness this gave to those who saw the Christian family in action.

This appreciation of the witness of Christian marriage and family, of course, helped it to address the fourth point it inherited from the scriptures. Marriage and family had a part to play in the work and mission of Jesus by making others aware of what a difference the Christian message could make in the daily chores of life. On a simpler level, the church could also appreciate the need for family in keeping the church going. New life was needed to fulfill the plan of salvation. It was also the family's task to educate its members in the Christian way of life.

NOTES

1. "The Letter of St. Clement to the Corinthians" in *Apostolic Fathers*, Francis X. Glimm, trans. (New York: Cima Publishing Co., 1947) pp. 9–10.

2. Quoted in Joseph Kerns, *The Theology of Marriage* (New York: Sheed and Ward, 1964) p. 31.

3. *Opus Imperfectum Contra Julianum*, Book 6, Chapter 30, in Kerns, p. 36.

4. Ibid., p. 37.

5. Kerns, p. 15.

6. "Commentary on the Literal Meaning of Genesis (Book 9, Chapter 7, n. 12)" in Theodore Mackin, *What Is Marriage?* (New York: Paulist Press, 1982) p. 129.

7. Edward Schillebeeckx, *Marriage* (New York: Sheed and Ward, 1965) p. 245.

STUDY QUESTIONS

1. What were the two basic choices faced in the patristic period?

2. Compare church responses to the cultural challenge in the second century and the sixteenth century. Why were the responses so different?

3. What is meant by dualism? Why did the church embrace it? Why is dualism important for understanding the Christian view of marriage?

4. What were the goods of marriage according to St. Augustine? What were the reservations he expressed about marriage?

5. How much regulation did the church during the patristic period exercise over marriage?

FURTHER STUDY

Kerns, Joseph. *The Theology of Marriage* (New York: Sheed and Ward, 1964). An excellent collection of quotations from different primary sources developed around different themes relating to marriage.

Mackin, Theodore. *The Marital Sacrament* (New York: Paulist Press, 1989). Traces the sense of marriage as a sacrament through history, including the patristic period discussed in this chapter.

———. *What Is Marriage?* (New York: Paulist Press, 1982). A history of the theology of marriage in the Catholic Church.

Saint Augustine. *Treatise on Marriage and Other Subjects*. Roy J. Deferrari, ed. (Washington: The Catholic University of America, 1955). Augustine has many pieces dealing with marriage. This work gives a sample.

Schillebeeckx, Edward. *Marriage* (New York: Sheed and Ward, 1965). A good short history of marriage in the church.

Stevenson, Kenneth. *Nuptial Blessing: A Study of Christian Marriage Rites* (New York: Oxford University Press, 1982). The patristic period is treated as part of a larger historical study.

5.

Marriage in the Medieval Period

———————— ◇ ————————

Aside from the growing sense of marriage as a sacrament, the medieval period does not offer any radical changes in the attitude of the church. What it does offer is a significant change in the practice of religion. As the Germanic tribes overran the western half of the Roman empire in the late fifth century, the order of society was seriously disrupted. More to the point, large numbers of people from the north of Europe, who had little or no education and who had little or no grasp of how to govern a complex society, descended upon the Mediterranean world.

While these people had much to dislike about their former Roman foes, they also had to admire them. They envied the Romans for their wealth, their power, and their stability. In many ways the new invaders tried to imitate the life and institutions of the defeated empire. They were not too successful. They often imitated the structure, but the heart of the lifestyle could not be captured again.

A good case in point can be found in the transformation of Christianity. In the centuries since his death, the followers of Jesus had grown in numbers, especially since AD 313, when Constantine gave the church official recognition. After the fall of the empire, Christian missionaries eagerly turned toward the large masses of Germanic people in hopes of converting them to the religion which the Germans associated with the empire. The missionaries were immensely successful in calling large numbers of these people to the church. However, once they were baptized, the new converts did not leave behind them the customs, beliefs, and practices of their former tribal life. Christianity certainly was successful in creating change in the lives of the newcomers. It in turn was changed by the converts.

As a result, Christianity in the thousand years following the fall of the Roman empire was a mixture of many elements. There was the tradition it inherited from the earlier members of its community. There were the beliefs and practices of the tribal life of its new converts. Finally, there were the peculiar practices developed during the middle ages themselves—from the latter part of the fifth century through a significant part of the fifteenth century. This blend of so many traditions made the fabric of the medieval church very different from its predecessor.

The change is no more evident than in the practice of family life. The Germanic tribes brought with them a strong sense of the special importance of the domestic unit. It was the family that passed on life. The family had a moving and magical power in their world.

Dualism (the sense of the spirit in conflict with the body) was too deeply entrenched in the church for it to share comfortably in the simple tribal adoration of the family. Besides, there was not much in the daily experience of disorder found in the "dark ages" to sing the praises of the domestic life. With the chaos of the times, it was quite easy to spurn this world in hopes of a better life in the spirit world. However, the folk religion of the time did not give up the indispensable position of the family's importance:

> European Christian families were left to develop domestic rites which combined pre-Christian beliefs and Christian rituals. . . . House blessings by priests increased fertility and protected the home from evil. Priests, unlike monks or bishops, had little theological education, and often married. They adapted their understanding of Christianity to fit their own needs or those of the local community.[1]

There are many examples of these domestic rituals that are available to the modern investigator. One very fruitful source is the record of the inquisition proceedings held under Jacques Fournier, bishop of Pamiers. The register compiled under his investigations gives a very detailed account of the proceedings and testimonies from 1318 to 1325 as the bishop tried to check the Albigensian movement in southern France.

One account tells how a local clergyman, believing in the special powers contained in the hair and nails of dead victims, wanted to protect the good fortune of his household after the death of his parents. He did not want the power of the house to leave with their entrance into the afterlife. The following account is found:

> When Pons Clergue, the priest's father, died, many people from the Pays d'Aillon came to the house of the priest, his son. The body was placed in the "house within the house," called the foganha (kitchen); it was not yet wrapped in a shroud; the priest then sent everyone out of

the house with the exception of Alazais Azema and Brune Pourcel, the bastard daughter of Prades Taverniler; the women remained alone with the dead man and the priest; the women and the priest took the locks of hair and bits of finger- and toe-nail from the corpse. . . . Later there was rumor that the priest had done the same with the corpse of his mother.[2]

What a plot for a class B movie! Imagine sitting in a drive-in theater (remember what they were!) on a stormy night with lightning and thunder popping all around. The script would not have to change much. Perhaps the scene should include a hunchback called Igor who slithers around assisting the priest in his ritual. Otherwise the scene could walk by itself into the annals of the Friday night specials.

To the modern mind, of course, the medieval priest sounds very strange. Hair and nails do continue to grow after brain death. Perhaps that is why there was such a concern that they be preserved. But why such a concern for the household?

To an extent the answer is quite easy. On the other hand it is quite difficult. These medieval people were so taken with the household because they drew their identity from the family. They did not think of themselves as separate from the blood ties that nurtured them. The world was alive with terrifying mystery. There were mysterious powers lurking around every bend in the road of life. The family clung together in a struggle to keep the powers of fortune in their lives.

In this sense the medievalist had a stronger grasp on the true power of family. In today's society, where many are taken with the power of the human to shape the world through the powers of technology, there are not for such people too many mysterious powers left. There are just unsolved problems. The present struggle is seen in many ways as taking place in a plastic world that can be reshaped provided humans learn enough about the world and how to control it.

In such a milieu the family becomes just one other reality that can be arranged according to the designs of human intention. If the family is dysfunctional, by all means present society feels it imperative that every effort be exercised to set it right. But if things do not work out to the satisfaction of everyone, then divorce has come to be accepted as the best solution. One simply picks up the pieces and proceeds to rebuild a new family unit with a mixture of new and old characters.

Such a plastic world was indeed foreign to the medieval people. To them the family truly came before the individual. The inquisition proceedings against the Albigensians that were mentioned above continue at one point with the struggles of a woman accused of heresy. As she considers confessing to the charges, she receives frantic counsel. The entry is curious because it does not focus on what will happen to her as a person as much as what will happen to her household:

> Vain and foolish woman! If you confess all these things, you will lose all your possessions and put out the fire of your house. Your children, their hearts full of anger, will go and beg alms. . . . Let the sleeping hare lie, take another path so as not to wake him, or he will wound your hands with his feet. . . . I can see an even better way to keep your house standing. For I, as long as the Lord Bishop shall live, will be of his house; and I can do much good; and I can give my daughter as wife to one of your sons. And so our house will be more successful, more comfortable.[3]

How horrible! If she confesses, she will "put out the fire of [her] . . . house." Why on earth would she be concerned with her household instead of her own life? That question is baffling to the modern individualist. To the medieval mind which saw identity coming from the family, the woman made perfect sense.

A. Tensions Facing the Church

The church faced a strong cult of the family among its newest members, and it was little prepared to meet such a passionate embrace of the domestic life. It had inherited from its own faith tradition a definite reserve about family life. The tradition emphasized the individual and the search for God; it accepted the battle between spirit and matter, and it championed the celibate life lived either in a monastic setting or within the more immediate life of the community church. How was it to meet the Germanic worship of family as the key to all life?

The tension was not easily resolved. Often it led to an hypocrisy as the people adjusted to the demands of the church on an official level only to devise their own peculiar practices in the push and shove of daily life. Such an adjustment clearly comes through in the inquisition hearings of those suspected of Albigensianism.

The medieval church's first reaction to the family lifestyle of its newest members was positive. The church's theology did not allow it to embrace the family as the highest calling within the Christian vocation. On a practical level, however, it did appreciate the need for a stable family life. The decline in values and stability in the closing days of the Roman empire left the church desperately looking for a lifestyle that would improve the practice of its ordinary member. The sense of family among the Germanic tribes appeared to be a welcomed change.

Honeymoons, however, do not last very long. The church soon discovered that the cult of the family was indeed a mixed blessing. The church's conflict with the domestic practices of the medieval period centered around several issues.

Feuding Families

Many of the more powerful families were intense units. With the breakdown of the central government, a seignorial or manorial system developed in which the society hung together through a network of powerful families controlling large tracts of land. These families would support a network or an alliance under a regional rule by supplying goods and services when necessary. These local landowners would in turn band together in a common effort as the need arose.

In many ways it was a tenuous network that depended on the good will or at least the fear of its members. Certainly when the more peculiar system known as feudalism developed, there were oaths of allegiance and more formal treaties. The reality, though, was that the claims of family needs often took precedence over any alliance or duty to the central cause.

Frequently family feuds would develop which would paralyze the functions of the society. When a member of a family would be slain or affronted, revenge was mandated. If the guilty individual could not be identified or reached, then any member of the offending family could be used as an adequate substitute. These feuds could, therefore, string along in an infinite fashion.

> The Church was more civilized than its . . . members, who still carried on ferocious feuds. In parts of Holland a murdered family member was not supposed to be buried until the family had avenged him. It was not necessary to kill the guilty party; another member of the offending family would do as well. This is what family solidarity meant in those days. Understandably, the Church supported monarchies that would attempt to control such feuds.[4]

These conflicts did not go along without having their impact on the daily life of society or the daily functions of the church. How could the parish conduct its common worship if the members were busy slaying each other? Even if matters were not at a fever pitch, the church often found itself frustrated in trying to nurture the sacramental life of its people as families would refuse to receive the sacraments together.

The net result would be, therefore, that the church and the families would often be at odds. The family had its honor to protect. The church had to nurture the common life of the community.

Infanticide

The family unit had to jealously protect its holdings. Not only must it meet the threats of the other families intent on cutting into its goods, but it had to guard against the corruption of the family unit from within. There were the obvious issues of too many children for the inheritance, illegitimate children, or severely handicapped children who could not contribute to the common good. There were also the less obvious issues that arose from the superstitions of the day. Twins or children with certain complexions were at times seen as the result of the devil's interference or of an adulterous relationship.

Whatever the reasons, infanticide was a common practice throughout the period. Precise numbers are impossible to determine, but the practice was persistent enough to be a constant source of conflict between the church and the families. The powerful families were trying to keep what they had. They struggled against diluting their holdings. The poorer families were often simply trying to keep from starvation. The church, on the other hand, had to constantly try to protect the rights and dignity of each person which its tradition insisted upon. None of God's children could be murdered.

Nepotism

Families were interested in positioning their children in society. The interest in the child was not primarily the simple joy of seeing one you love succeed. Individuals were to serve the interest of the family. They were placed in positions of power whenever possible so that they could help the family. Obviously, conflicts of interests were frequent where the common good demanded one thing from a person in office and the demands of the family beckoned for a different course of action. This tension between the duties of office and the duties toward family is no clearer than with placement of family members in the church.

The church held tremendous power in medieval society. All families were interested in having their representatives in the religious orders which had such large land holdings and wealth. They were also interested in having family members well placed in the secular (non-monastic) clergy. Bishoprics were especially valued since they often had such power and wealth.

There was thus a double material value in placing the family's younger children or illegitimate children in church service. First, there was the wealth and the power of the church that well-placed members could use for the benefit of their families of origin. Second, the church could serve as a refuge for unwanted family members who would simply dissipate the family's wealth. With younger and illegitimate children placed in the church, they would not lay claim to any of the family inheritance.

Families, however, were not simply interested in shipping their children off to the church for material benefits. They had very sincere religious motives for placing their members in the church. Medieval people genuinely believed in the power of the spiritual world. They were convinced that a member in a cloistered monastery or nunnery could be of invaluable aid to the family. The prayers they sent heavenward for the good of the family could not be dismissed. The power of God was real, and those close to God would not be denied.

The epidemics of the age left no doubt about the need for supernatural protection. There certainly was no effective protection on this earth against the plagues that regularly besieged Europe. There were just so many mysterious powers operative in the world—from weather to disease—that one did not question the powers of the religious forces. To have a spokesperson present in the heart of the church representing the interests of the family was clearly a significant need.

From the church's perspective, then, the desire to place family members into religious positions was not all bad. The problem the church had with this nepotism was that its own interests and values were threatened. People who had little or no interest in religious or priestly life could be forced into vows by their families. The end result was unhappy people who often did not live up to their vows.

The church needed sincerity in its leaders. It struggled against families by first barring illegitimate children from some offices. It also tried to ensure that people freely selected their vocation. The church and the family, then, were often at odds over the rights of the individual.

Age of Marriage

For a number of reasons which will be treated in subsequent pages, the church insisted that marriage took place only when the couple freely committed themselves to each other. It insisted that a boy or a girl had to be of sufficiently mature years before they had the judgment that allowed for proper consent. It also insisted that marriage was primarily for procreation. Therefore, the people in question had to be of sufficient physical maturity to allow for the proper completion of the marriage act.

For many of the families, however, marriage was primarily for social and economic reasons. Marriages were arranged to secure the well-being of the family. Frequently the good of the family demanded that the marriage be arranged early in the life of the child.

There were many reasons for pre-arranging marriages at an early age. Some were arranged when the children were only two or three years old. The reasons may not be readily understood today when the strongest motivation for marriage is romantic love. People today are in search of a soul mate. Nature, in a sense, is seen as having designed an excellent complement for each of us. Many walk around with the idea that "some enchanted evening you may see a stranger across a crowded room." The song from *South Pacific* continues that "somehow you'll know" that this stranger is the person meant by nature to be one's spouse or lover. How one knows is not quite clear. Perhaps the tell-tale signal is the tingle that runs up and down the spine. Somehow, though, one is supposed to be convinced that a given person is one's true soul mate.

There are those, of course, who have gone past the pangs of romantic love. People who are in a stable marriage probably have come to realize that after a joyous, envious, painful period of romantic love, they have to settle down to learn how to love the other. Love that endures the ebb and flow of life fully recognizes the acne, underarm problems, and personality warps of the other. This type of love is a broader notion of two people committing themselves to each other "for better and for worse." It is a commitment that must eagerly warm its hands on the glowing embers of romantic love and which must rejoice at the occasional flare of the flame. It is a commitment that struggles to feed on the quiet pleasures of a child's first step or the thrill of still being able to walk together in the twilight years. It is a commitment, though, which requires that one be able to look at the other and see ugliness and insecurity without turning heel.

In either case marriage today is looking for love or its more modest cousin, companionship. A modern marriage cannot easily understand a relationship that stresses the domestic setting primarily for social and economic reasons. In medieval times the church told its members that they had the duty to love the other once married. No doubt there were love relationships that did develop. No doubt, with such a limited emphasis on personal choice, there were many marriages that were steeped in anger.

Medieval families, however, were faced with many threats. Fewer than twenty-five percent of the population would make it to their twenty-fifth year. Even after escaping the threatening clouds of childhood diseases, life was quite precarious with plagues sweeping away over half the population in some regions. The Black Death of the fourteenth century, for example, wiped out between twenty and forty-five percent of the total European population.[5] Combine that single source of death with the myriad other threats facing exposed, fragile human life, and one begins to understand the desperate situation faced by families.

When the father of a family died, the destiny of the family would frequently fall into the hands of outsiders. The poor peasants, of course, were always at the mercy of the owners of the fiefs. They were bought and sold with the land. While there were many degrees of distinction in the early medieval period among the different levels of peasants, most would appear to the modern perspective to be in slavery of one degree or another. The peasants fought for their rights, and over the period of the thousand medieval years from the fifth century to the fifteenth century, they made impressive gains. But at most points in the history of the period, a family left without the father would be pushed to the edge of existence.

Families of the nobility fared better, of course. Likewise, when the middle class began to make its appearance toward the end of the medieval period with the growth of urban centers, they devised ways of caring for their families. But the threat to the families of even these more stable groups was real.

In areas where the feudal system developed, for example, the nobility governed huge tracts of land. In return they had the obligation to provide the king with men and supplies for the wars and well-being of the nation. The mother was not seen as fit to carry out this task. Another man had to step in and replace the deceased father and govern the family. At times the appointed man might be a relative. At other times the wardship was sold to the highest bidder. Understandably, then, families wanted to solidify their positions as soon as possible through the early advantageous marriage of their children with other families. These marriages would place some restrictions on the conduct of future wards.

Middle class people had some protection through their guilds. These professional organizations often governed the arrangements and demanded accountability of any guardian over a family of one of their former members. Still, one can understand how the family would like to make its own choices and form its own alliance as soon as possible. The odds were very great that the male parent would die before the children would grow to adulthood.

As sympathetic as the church might be to the interests of the family, its theology of marriage had to insist on the free consent of the parties entering the marriage. First, it had to insist that the children be old enough to comprehend what was being promised. The church, probably taking its lead from Roman law, demanded that the girl be at least twelve years of age and that the boy be at least fourteen years old. It did not recognize marriages as valid if they were contracted by younger parties unless the marriage was actually consummated by sexual relations. Second, it passed a number of laws designed to ensure that parties were not coerced into marriages at an older age. Such laws were not easy to enforce. When does social pressure negate true individual choice?

There were, of course, other conflicts between the church and the family. These are simply the more dramatic ones and give a taste of the types of issues which the church and the families had to face in dealing with each other.

The Marriage Contract

At the beginning of the medieval period the church was faced with difficult questions about the contractual reality of marriage. As in the patristic period, the church did not take a very active part in governing marriages. Christians followed the laws of their region which governed the practice of marriage. The church community offered its exhortation as to the virtues and purposes of marriage. There were certain practices which it generally did not recognize, such as divorce, and other practices upon which it frowned, such as remarriage. Finally, it did create some rules governing the marriage of clergy. All in all, however, it did not enter the marriage business.

With the middle ages, however, the church found itself in the midst of a society that struggled for the basic stability of life. Often that society turned to the church to serve as a representative of civil authority. Where the church functioned in that role, it was thrust into the thorny legal questions governing marriage.

The church also found itself presented with many different concepts of what constituted marriage. The Roman tradition which it embraced for so many years had its norms. But the new ruling people had their tribal customs which were often at odds with those of their Roman predecessors.

Marriage remained a secular practice throughout the greater part of the period. Christians were not required to have the church officiate at their services until the eleventh century. But the church was constantly pressed to decide what were valid marriages. In its function as arbitrator, it was continually called upon to determine the civic obligations of this or that party. It also had to counsel what was sinful practice and what was not. Finally, if marriage created an unbreakable bond between spouses, when did that bond take place? When were the two people irreversibly linked to each other?

There were several practices surrounding the initiation of marriage at the beginning of the period:

1. From the Roman practice, marriage took place simply with the consent of the two parties. The exchange of promises could take place in private or in public.

2. There was the practice of the exchange of gifts. The practice varied from one tribe—Vandals, Franks, Lombards, etc.—to another. Each practice, such as the bride's family giving a gift or the groom giving the gift to the bride's family, had a slightly different meaning from tribe to tribe. Almost invariably it designated marriage as a contract between the families.

3. There were the practices of different ceremonies surrounding the joining of the two parties and the two families. Frequently these ceremonies were highlighted by the exchange of vows. Often, though, they were preceded by the exchange of promises dealing with matters other than the personal commitment of the married couple.

4. There was the emphasis placed on handing the bride over to the groom or the bride being taken across the threshold of the new home. Such ceremonies indicated that the bride took up residence in the new family. In a sense this was often seen as the consummation of the contract begun in the exchange of gifts.

5. There was the obvious emphasis on the first act of intercourse as the beginning or the consummation of the marriage.

The question facing the church was: When did marriage take place? It was an important question for the church. It was a question it had to face as the civil arbitrator. It was also a question it had to face in the daily rhythm of its own internal concerns. In meeting its challenge, the church seemed to combine the sense of the supernatural with the sense of the legal. It spoke of an indispensable, mysterious bond that was sealed in heaven by a given act performed through the power of the church. The question the church had to face, of course, was at what point did that seal, which would bind the couple irreversibly to each other, take effect.

Obviously, the many practices of marriage among its various people did not make it easy for the church to define a single act as the moment when marriage took place. There was a minefield of delicate politics threatening any acceptable answer. As powerful as the church was, it could not simply impose its will on the varied people who embraced Christianity. As earlier quotes showed, folk religion had a will of its own.

The church's thinking was shaped by the culture which cradled it. The confusions of the time were its confusions. It had the richness of its tradition to navigate through some of the turmoil. It felt it had the guidance of the Spirit in meeting the challenges of the day. Nevertheless, it is still obvious just how much of its thinking was indebted to its age.

The church had a natural affinity for the Roman approach which saw mutual consent as the start of marriage. Its theology emphasized the dignity of the individual. It compared the marital bond to that existing between Christ and the church. The scriptures repeatedly emphasized that the people of God were free in their response of love and service. There had to be some sense of freedom for the marriage commitment to be meaningful.

Certainly the Roman approach with its emphasis on mutual consent was preferable to the sense of contract found so often in the tribal customs which emphasized the exchange of gifts. Often these contractual views of marriage placed the man in control of the woman. They blurred even the rudiments of mutuality which were necessary to preserve the goods of marriage as enunciated by Augustine and the sense of companionship found in the scriptures.

There were, however, serious practical problems in accepting only the mutual exchange of promises between the couple as the essence of marriage. Society could not function very well if there was not a public witness or ceremony so often demanded by tribal practices. On the one hand, if marriage did not require a public ceremony or public witnesses, either of the parties could simply deny the promise was ever made. On the other hand, children who were faced with an arranged marriage which they did not wish to honor could simply claim a prior secret marriage. Such a claim could be made even after a public ceremony if second thoughts arose for either the bride or the groom. Either party could invalidate the ceremonies and the contracts of the family by claiming to have been married secretly before such public agreements took place.

Secret marriages made it very difficult for the normal life of the society to function in a reasonable way. Whatever guidelines the church devised in its role as arbitrator of public life, it had to take into consideration the texture of daily life. Thus, it faced similar problems if the questions of impotence or sterility were entirely removed from the picture. Families could be left without any offspring, and the bride or the groom left without a sex partner. Neither practice would be readily received by the folk patterns of the day.

Toward the end of the medieval period, then, the church arrived at a practice which showed its continued preference for marriage as being anchored in the mutual consent of the parties involved. However, it combined this pivotal element with acknowledgements of the importance of public ceremony and sexual intercourse as it faced the issues of impediments to marriage and the challenges of consummated marriages. The exchange of vows, in other words, was the essence of marriage, but the vows had to be exchanged in the proper setting, by the proper people, and followed by the appropriate sexual activity before they would be recognized as lawful and consummated. The church held that it could declare that the improper exchange of vows was not binding.

B. The Theology of Marriage

Jesus called marriage good. Scripture called it good. In fact the New Testament in Ephesians 5 links the bond of marriage in a special way with the work of Jesus in the church. The patristic period had to follow their lead and recognize the good of marriage. The mainstream medieval church, therefore, could not abandon the honored place of marriage. However, as the previous section showed, the dualistic worldview that dominated the thinking of the earliest centuries of the church remained intact during the middle ages. As a result, the church's acceptance of marriage during this period often appears as a very reluctant consent to the norms set down by the tradition.

There was little in the medieval experience which would cause it to question the dualism that served as the setting for early Christian reflection. There was little in the experience of medieval people which would move them to sing the glories of the physical world or to see the physical and the spiritual as being on a continuum.

Daily life in the chaos that followed the fall of the Roman empire was difficult. The new Germanic peoples who controlled much of the western half of the former empire had none of the broad organizational, economic, or political skills that their predecessors had and which were necessary to govern a large territory. As a result, the quality of everyday living noticeably deteriorated.

It was pointed out in an earlier part of this chapter that the first system to develop in the vacuum following the fall of the Roman government was a system of seignorial lands or large manors. A powerful family or leader would simply control an area and try to govern the economic life of the people in the region. It was primarily an economy of goods and services. People would be permitted to work a piece of land. In return for the permission to work the land and for a certain amount of protection, the people were supposed to supply goods and services to the main house.

Out of this economic structure there arose in the eighth and ninth centuries a military and political system which could be termed more precisely feudal. The power which achieved military dominance of an area would grant a fief to the leading military men who helped achieve the power. They in return would hold the fief as long as they would pledge allegiance to the ruler granting the holdings.

The bottom line of both the seignorial system and the feudal system was a strongly hierarchical form of life. There was the ruling class of nobles with many distinctions within their ranks. There were the peasants with their numerous classes of distinction.

Most of the peasants had to earn a living off at best twenty-five to thirty acres of land. These lands that they were able to work were called tributary lands. In return for this privilege to work the lands, the peasant was required to work for three or more days a week the seignorial lands. As a result the wife and the children had to carry many of the burdens of tending the family's tributary plot from which they had to earn their livelihood.

The cruelty of life can only be appreciated if one tries to reconstruct the particulars of daily existence. The facts available are not abundant, but one can use them to probe under the fabric of life. The peasant lived in a dirt-floored mud hut. It was about thirty feet long and usually did not have any windows. The roof was generally made of a thatch weaved from the corn and wheat crops. Smoke from the home fires in the winter months was usually allowed to escape through holes left near the eaves. In certain areas there is evidence that these houses were shared by some of the animals which were so important for the continuance of life.

With such conditions it is not hard to see why life was fragile. Disease, death, and poverty limited the size of each household. The total number of adults and children usually did not exceed five. If the households got any larger, they probably could not support themselves. As it was the diet was a very meager one.

Thirty acres with modern farming methods could possibly produce the necessities of life. However, these people did not have either the luxury of modern farming or the benefit of their total crop yield. They were at the mercy of every drought and agricultural pest that existed. They had few if any weapons to fight the flux of plenty and famine that usually visits natural farming methods. Even if they had a good year, they still had to give a sizable portion of their yield to the main house in return for the privilege of cultivating the land.

Every privilege required a return in goods and services. If the peasant wanted to graze an animal on the pasture lands of the seignorial holdings, then a price had to be paid in terms of animals or some other food. Even the fish and game of the rivers and countryside were not free to be used. They belonged to the main owner of the lands.

All this resulted in a very meager diet which one author summarized in the following terms:

> There can be little doubt that the mass of the population lived primarily on a carbohydrate diet consisting mainly of foodstuffs and drink made from barley and oats. . . . In addition, a few peas and beans provided a leguminous element in the diet, which was made tastier principally by the addition of onions and garlic. Although the protein content of the peasant and workman's diet in the fifteenth century may have been fairly high, this was certainly not true in the thirteenth century. Meat and cheese were scarce because livestock was scarce.[6]

Life for the upper classes was probably better in many ways. However, one must realize that the plagues and death that awaited the general population did not know class distinction. Furthermore, the upper classes did not have much if any privacy. Their houses were public houses in which the business of the lands was carried out. There were few if any private rooms. Households, including servants and guests, gathered around a common fire at night in their attempt to keep warm.

Chimneys were not commonplace until the close of the period. It was difficult to have specialized or private rooms since they could not benefit from the main fire. In fact, the history of furniture would indicate that the main house on the seignorial manse was a large hall used for many different functions throughout the day. There were no specialized dining rooms or bedrooms. Eating tables or beds were usually folded away during most of the day and assembled only when needed.

This long digression into the daily life of the medieval world is necessary to understand why the forces promoting the domestic life were not strong enough to break the hold that dualism had on the thinking of the church. Dualism today is rejected primarily for two reasons. First, all of our probings of the world continually insist that there is an inherent link between the growth of our spirit and the physical conditions that surround us. Soul and body, spirit and matter are not opposed. On the contrary, they are irrevocably linked to each other.

The second reason for renouncing dualism comes from a more immediate experience of the world. People today, at least the majority in the first world countries and a significant number in developing nations, generally have a positive encounter with the physical world. They have decent clothes, good food, and adequate housing. There is usually access to flowers, and colors, and a basic security. Even where such goods are not a reality in a person's life, there are enough images and examples of it that one frequently has hope. In such a setting it is difficult to be dualistic.

The medieval experience, however, was brutal enough that there was not sufficient motivation to spurn the dualism it inherited. Not only were the material goods of the world severely limited, but the chaos and injustice that the typical person experienced in life was directly attributable to the unwieldy drives of people. Lust for power, avarice, gluttony, envy, hatred, jealousy, and the sexual appetites were easily seen as the source of the disorder prevalent in the world. These appetites, these emotions were seen as emanating primarily from the bodily drives seeking fulfillment. Clearly, life would only improve to the extent that people were taught a life of self-control. They had to check their baser drives.

The medieval church maintained the dualistic worldview that it inherited from the patristic period. As a result, it saw the celibate life as the way of perfection. The married life was a lower calling which was in fact extended to the majority of the church.

Marriage was necessary to continue the race since death was introduced after the fall. Even within marriage one was called to continence and self-control. One could only engage in the sex act for the explicit purpose of procreation. Any deliberate enjoyment of the carnal pleasures would be catering to the bodily appetites in the worst way. Few, if any, were seen as capable of resisting the powerful pleasures of the sexual drive. In fact, then, the sexual act was seen as a source of sin.

This was the position taken among official circles and in the theological debates of the day. It was, in the main, the line of argument and reasoning the period inherited. One author, Joseph E. Kerns, offers an interesting challenge to how widespread such a teaching was among the common people. He points out that few could read the exchanges among the male celibates who dominated the church's theological writings. Furthermore, he argues, there is little or no evidence that the sinfulness of the sexual act within marriage was presented to the people in either the sermons of the day or in the confessionals.[7]

The existing sermons dwell on many topics. One would expect them to dwell on something as important as the issues of domestic life. Why is

the need for restraint in marriage, more particularly the need to renounce all venereal pleasure between husband and wife, not featured in
existing sermons? Kerns might be right in his insistence that people were
simply left to live their lives and not bothered with what was seen as an
inevitable course of human behavior. The one fly in the ointment is that
most of the sermons that still exist today were those given at important
events, and most of those would not center on domestic questions. There
is no way of knowing what was said in the dilapidated chapel to the
Saxon peasants.

Kerns does seem to be on stronger ground when he argues that the
penitentials do not elaborate on the sinfulness of the marital act. These
penitentials were books which listed sins on one side and the appropriate penance on the other. They were manuals written to help the
uneducated clergy administer the sacrament of penance. They were
quite free in listing any type of sin. The absence of any sin dealing with
intercourse within marriage would be significant.

The church in its pastoral approach may have softened its dualistic
base in teaching about marriage. There is little evidence, however, that
within theological circles the edge of criticism was blunted. The dualism
was intact. The suspicions about the efficacy of marriage for promoting
the life of Christian perfection was also intact.

There are, however, two significant changes found toward the end
of the period. There is a change in the way marriages take place and in
the basic idea of what happens during the marriage ceremony. In a sense
the first, the change in practice, contributes to the change in the theology
of marriage.

As previously reported, the earliest Christians did not practice any
peculiar marriage rite. They simply followed the customs of the day and
of the area in which they lived. There was a sense of being married "in
the Lord." As Christians, in other words, they had a vision of life that
was expected to carry over into their entire life. Certainly the Christian
vision of life should be present in marriage which served as such a
cornerstone for their entire life.

It is more than an accident that once marriage became entrenched
as a liturgical ceremony in the church, the thinking about marriage underwent significant developments. The changes in thinking between
the eleventh and the thirteenth centuries were truly developments
and not radically new approaches. They were, however, significant
developments.

Before the close of the middle ages marriage was accepted as one of
the seven sacraments of the church. St. Augustine, of course, whose
thought was so influential from the earliest period of the middle ages,

spoke of marriage as a *sacramentum*. Building upon passages such as the one found in Ephesians 5, he felt that marriage established a special bond between the partners. In turn he argued that living out this bond in a faithful way gave witness to the world of the commitment that existed between Christ and his church. Marriage then was of significant importance in the life of the Christian.

The development among the scholastic theologians (a name given to the systematic theology of the time because it developed in the scholastic atmosphere of the cathedral school or the university) of the medieval period did not deny Augustine's position. In building upon it, they argued that marriage not only signified the bond between the husband and the wife, it created it. The marriage sacrament, drawing upon the power of the church, created a reality that would exist between the husband and wife which could never be dissolved.

One author tries to capture the difference in thinking between the approach of the early church and the later development among the scholastic theologians in the following terms:

> According to the church Fathers the dissolution of marriage was not *permissible;* but according to the schoolmen its dissolution was not *possible.*[8]

The sacred action of the wedding ceremony according to this way of thinking created a mystical reality that even the church could not undo. Such an approach to marriage left it indeed in a strange situation during the ensuing centuries. Couched in the dualism of the day, marriage was seen as a lower way of Christian life when compared to the celibate calling. It was a comparison that remained in force in the Catholic Church until the Second Vatican Council in the middle of this century. On the other hand marriage was one of the seven sacraments of the church and as such must indeed be important in the eyes of God. Even the celibates did not have a sacrament to confer graces upon their lifestyle unless they entered the priesthood.

NOTES

1. Colleen McDannell, *The Christian Home in Victorian America, 1840–1900* (Bloomington: Indiana University Press, 1986) p. 3.

2. Emmanuel LeRoy Ladurie, *Montaillous: The Promised Land of Error*, Barbara Bray, trans. (New York: Vintage Books, 1979) pp. 31–32.

3. Ibid., p. 25.

4. John Sommerville, *The Rise and Fall of Childhood* (Beverly Hills: Sage Publications, 1982) p. 59.

5. William H. McNeill, *Plagues and Peoples* (Garden City, New York: Anchor Books, 1976) p. 149.

6. R.H. Hilton, *A Medieval Society* (New York: John Wiley and Sons, Inc., 1966) p. 111.

7. Kerns, pp. 65–66.

8. Schillebeeckx, p. 284.

STUDY QUESTIONS

1. What was the German attitude toward family? How did the church respond?

2. What role did the family play in the identity of the individual in medieval society?

3. What were some of the points that caused tension between the church and the medieval family?

4. How did the church incorporate the many different ideas of marriage that it faced in the medieval period?

5. What did the medieval church mean by marriage as a sacrament? How was its understanding a significant development within the Christian tradition?

6. Why is it important to understand the daily life of the medieval family in assessing the church's attitude toward marriage?

FURTHER STUDY

Aries, Phillippe. *Centuries of Childhood* (New York: Vantage Books, 1962). A groundbreaking study of how the rearing of children was influenced by many areas including religion. It is not without its challenges in modern scholarship. It still makes fascinating reading.

Hilton, R.H. *A Medieval Society* (New York: John Wiley and Sons, Inc., 1966). To understand the religious thinking of a people, one must capture the rhythms of daily life in a period.

Ladurie, Emmanuel LeRoy. *Montaillous: The Promised Land of Error*, Barbara Bray, trans. (New York: Vintage Books, 1979). A book that allows the layperson to enter the fabric of a period as the people respond to the investigation of the Albigensians.

Mackin, Theodore. *The Marital Sacrament* (New York: Paulist Press, 1989). Studies the idea of sacrament in the medieval period as part of a larger historical work.

———— *What Is Marriage?* (New York: Paulist Press, 1982). A history of the theology of marriage in the Catholic Church.

Sommerville, John. *The Rise and Fall of Childhood* (Beverly Hills: Sage Publications, 1982). Gives a readable account of the various views of raising children.

6.

Marriage in the Reformation

———————— ◇ ————————

The reformation was a movement that was ready to happen. It was not only a question that there were lifestyles and practices in the church that begged to be changed because they did not live up to the call of Jesus. It was a question of realizing the importance of culture once again. The structures of the church in the sixteenth century were the product in many ways of the medieval culture. The imperial papacy, the sense of the quasi-magical that was often mixed with the legitimate sense of the mystical, the rigid sense of hierarchy and authority, the lack of respect for the individual conscience—these were understandable developments in the medieval church. They were not realities that sat well with the changes gradually taking hold of western culture in the sixteenth century, particularly in the northern and western parts of Europe. Basic changes had been in the making for quite some time.

To argue that the change introduced in the reformation was inevitable is not to say that the Protestants were right and that the Catholics were wrong. No reputable scholar would ever argue so simplistically. The web of the reformation was very complex. It is clear that the Protestant movement let much of the wisdom of the medieval church slip through its fingers in its rush to find a better expression of Christianity. Still, many of the significant changes championed by the reformers were predictable and inevitable.

The changes that took place in the sixteenth century may be viewed with a certain reasonableness by people with the comfortable perspective of four centuries. However, for the people who had to live through them, the changes were quite traumatic and volatile, especially the changes surrounding the practice and attitude toward the family.

In one sense the whole dynamic of the reformation would thrust the new groups into the arms of the family. The new order questioned the practice of celibacy, the monastic way of life, and the powerful hierarchical structure of the church which served as the foundation for so much of the medieval Christian's self-understanding.

Many of the leaders of the reformation were initially in religious orders, and part of their drive was to challenge the celibate way of life as a superior calling. Some of the reformers' statements did not rule out living in religious orders and congregations. However, they strongly resisted assigning a special charism to the calling. They refused to elevate the celibate way of life over the married vocation. Such an attempt at balance can be found in the Second Helvetic Confession (1566) which comes from the followers of Zwingli, one of the leading reformers in Switzerland:

> Those who have the gift of celibacy from heaven, so as to be pure and continent from their whole heart, may serve the Lord in that vocation in simplicity and humility, without exalting themselves above others.[1]

This statement clearly warns those who choose to remain virgins not to think of themselves as better simply because they choose not to marry. The Protestant tradition sees the call to perfection being extended to all Christians or at least to all the elect.

The Confession goes on to comment about marriage in the following terms:

> Marriage . . . was instituted by God, who blessed it richly, and inseparably joined man and woman to live together in intimate love and harmony (Matt xix.5). Marriage is honorable in all, and the bed is undefiled (Heb xiii.4; 1 Cor vii.28).[2]

For other leaders of the new religious movements, the balance of this statement was seen as too mild. One simply has to look at the statements by Martin Luther to see a more impassioned stance on the preference of marriage. In many ways, Luther, the ex-Augustinian monk, had a natural attraction to the family. One author captures this religious leader's personal position quite well:

> In place of the "counsels of perfection" being applied only to a few who were called to a higher life that included virginity, Luther rejected the idea of second-class status for any of the baptized. He found marriage to be the good and normal way of life, and the family a school of faith. In the family, he said, one daily practices the grace-full life of loving service as in no other living arrangement.[3]

Luther did not stop at calling the lay person to the height of the Christian calling. There were times when he clearly placed that calling in the home and not in any institutional church. At one point he addresses the choice of the mother:

> If a mother of a family wishes to please and serve God, let her not do what the papists are accustomed to doing: running to churches, fasting, counting prayers, etc. But let her care for the task in the kitchen . . . if she does these things in faith in the Son of God, and hopes that she pleases God on account of Christ, she is holy and blessed.[4]

Part of the spirit of Protestantism, in other words, was to play down the role of the church as an intermediary between the individual and God. Ideally the individual would use scripture as the main source of guidance. Different forms of Protestantism emphasized a variety of ecclesiologies or theories of the church. In general, however, there was less emphasis on the need for the church to intervene through its special powers.

This was the source of Luther's praising the work of the housewife. He did not want her to be like the "papists" with their "running to churches, fasting, counting prayers. . . ."

Others in the Protestant tradition were also enthusiastic in their support of the family as a center of religious practice. Many of the authors equated the home with some form of the church. Religious practice was not only assumed but in many instances demanded. While Luther encouraged the father to read the scriptures and administer baptism where there was a shortage of ministers,[5] the Puritans, for example, expected the head of the household to hold services as a matter of course. The strong imperative placed on the father is captured in the following terms:

> A special caste of priests no longer mediated between God and man: the residuary legatee was (or in the puritan view should be) the father of the family. He for God only, they for God in him. The man who shirked these responsibilities, still committing his conscience to a priest, Milton compared to a trader who handed all his business concerns over to a factor and lived merely on the profit without working himself.[6]

But this championing of family must not be taken on too simple a level. The relationship was complex, and as years passed, the honeymoon came to an end. The flow of daily life brought certain theological implications to the surface. The reformers eventually recognized complications that their early enthusiasm would not admit.

To begin with, the reformers generally made a distinction between the levels of church membership or affiliation. In New England, for example, one finds the Puritans approving the Halfway Covenant to address the declining membership in the churches. Meeting at the First Church in Boston in March 1662, church representatives agreed to extend baptism

> to the children of godly persons who were not full church members, that is, who had not experienced grace but had been baptized themselves and who professed an intellectual faith and submitted to church discipline.[7]

In this action which brought so much controversy in its day, a clear example of the tension or at least the distinction that existed between the church and the home can be found. Also, it can be seen that the religious experience, while nurtured by the Christian home, was essentially an individual one. Full membership in the church was originally limited to individuals who experienced a special grace. In addition to these full members there were two other classes. There were baptized people who were not members of the church, and there were those who regularly attended church, prayed in the congregation and at home, but were neither church members nor baptized.

Obviously, then, no matter how important and integral the family was to the life of the church, there was a clear distinction between the two. As a matter of fact there are evident signs that even among the reformers there were situations where the family was seen as a threat.

On the one hand, there are authors who would speak of the family as "a kind of a church" or describe the family worship in which the "priest-like father reads the sacred page," and where preachers would speak of the family as "a little church, a little state."[8] On the other hand, there was a clear movement to limit the father to the services within his own family. Where a father was found to take on ministerial functions outside of his family, he was quickly called to order. John Etherington, for example, "was fined and imprisoned by the High Commission on a charge of expounding the Scripture to others besides his own family" in 1626.[9] As early as 1583 the Puritans had prohibited "all preaching, reading, catechism and other such-like exercises in private places and families whereunto others do resort, being not of the same family."[10]

The question, then, is complicated. Even those churches which have the greatest motives for championing the family, if not identifying with it, pulled back and expressed reservations. Seldom were the church and the family simply seen as identical. As a matter of fact, one author shows that in the Protestant tradition the church and the home were not always placed on the same level or order of creation:

> In Protestant theology, the family has often been discussed within the dialectic of the orders of creation and redemption—that is, the way things basically are as God created the world and the way God in Jesus Christ has begun to transform all things from their fallen state. And the family in Protestant thought has sometimes been considered as belonging to the order of creation and not to the order of redemption.[11]

A. The Protestant Theology of Marriage

The one distinct development in the theology of marriage during the medieval period was to acknowledge marriage as one of the basic sacraments of the church. As such the marriage ceremony itself was seen as a source of a special grace or blessing from God. The sacrament of marriage was seen as creating a special supernatural reality which the church through its powers had the ability to bring into being. Once the church was instrumental in bringing the bond into being, however, it did not have the power to undo it. Once the bond was in place, no power on earth could void it.

Such an approach to marriage is understandable given the character of the medieval church. The following are a few points that were established in the previous section and should be highlighted again because they help in understanding the reaction of the Protestant churches.

1. Central governments were weak throughout most of the medieval period. The church grew in strength as the strongest international body. As such it controlled more and more facets of life. The church was slowly drawn into developing a complicated body of laws governing marriages.

2. People during the medieval period easily gravitated toward the superstitious, the magical, and the supernatural. There was a natural tendency to speak about sacred acts that created supernatural realities. While the church resisted the magical and superstitious, it did not go unaffected especially when the growth in superstition aided the power of the institutional church. Where the early Christian tradition was content with speaking of personal realities and obligations, there was a tendency in medieval theology to make supernatural realities that could be created or dismissed by acts of the church.

3. Where once divorce *was not* permitted because of the commitment expected on the part of Christians, now divorce *could not* be

permitted because of a distinct supernatural reality beyond the power of the church which had been created with the sacrament of marriage.

4. Given the entrenched dualism of the day, marriage was seen as a lesser calling despite the cult of family that existed among so many of the newly converted Germanic tribes. The celibate way of life was the highest calling for any Christian.

How did these realities sit with the reformation movement? What was the reformation movement about? No easy answer to either of these questions can do justice to such a complex reality. However, a few considerations can set the stage for understanding the Protestant approach to marriage.

First, the reformation was about power, autonomy, and a growing sense of individual freedom. Western culture had come to a point where it cherished more and more the ability of the person to decide the course of one's individual life. The more removed and persuasive power of scripture was preferred to the more immediate and imposing power of the church.

Second, the reformation was heavily influenced by ex-nuns and ex-priests. They were the natural religious leaders of their time. As they left the monasteries and the convents, they readily gravitated toward marriage and family. In a sense the family filled a void. If the celibate life was not going to be singled out as the ideal, then it was natural to see the call for perfection going out to all Christians.

Third, the culture as a whole began a slow journey of sliding away from a supernatural sense of reality. In other words, it had begun the secular process. To the secular mind, there may be depth and mystery in the present world. There is, however, only one reality. There is not a supernatural world over and distinct from the natural one.

Of course, the Protestant churches of the sixteenth century did not become loosely joined associations of secular humanists. Measured even by today's more conservative churches, the sixteenth century counterparts would appear to be quite authoritative, quite puritanical, and highly supernatural. However, from the vantage of four centuries, it is clear how many of the patterns in the Protestant churches were anchored in a persistent movement in the culture. There were in the movements of the day recognizable steps in asserting the rights of the individual conscience, a more egalitarian or at least collegial notion of the church, and an insistence on the continuity or oneness of all reality.

But the question for this study must be how all these movements came to focus on the question of marriage. What impact did the shift from a more authoritative, centralized church and a willingness to speak of supernatural realities have on the theory and practice of marriage? Clearly, the most dramatic change in the Protestant movement is its rejection of marriage as a sacrament. Marriage was not a sacrament in the New Testament, the reformers argued. Likewise, one could not find substantial support in the fathers of the church. No, they argued, the sense of sacrament that the sixteenth century church inherited was the creation of medieval theologians and not a natural conclusion of a sense of reality deeply entrenched in the tradition as the Catholic Church would argue.

It was not that the Protestant theologians wanted to belittle marriage. On the contrary they placed it in an honored position. In some respects it was considered more important than in the Catholic Church. It was no longer a lesser calling. It was the height of the Christian vocation. However, Protestants were suspicious of any changes that took place in the medieval period. They were also suspicious of anything that would place the church in the role of an indispensable intermediary between the individual and God. A major concern on the part of the Protestant movement was to appeal to the authority of scripture over what it felt were distortions that entered into the church, especially during the medieval period.

When it looked at scripture, the reformed movement did not find any evidence that Jesus set out to establish seven sacraments or that marriage was essentially different in the New Testament than in the Old. The conclusion, as far as Protestant thinkers were concerned, was that marriage was simply part of God's plan from the very beginning of the Old Testament. It was a natural institution which brought its participants the strength of God's help as they lived their life in commitment and fidelity to each other.

In their minds, Jesus did not establish a new form of marriage. Rather, his intent was to call his followers back to the original ideal of the Old Testament. He demanded that his followers live in constant fidelity.

To understand the Protestant position on the question of sacrament, it is necessary to realize the persistent struggle the church experienced in developing the proper perspective on marriage. Each age—the New Testament era, the patristic period, the medieval church, the Protestant movement—was convinced that the married way of life was a graced way of life. It was an approved way of life in which God was active in the relationship. However, this sense of marriage being in the flow of God's generosity to the world was tempered or balanced with a sense that a special relationship between the individual and God made all other relationships pale.

In the New Testament the tension can be seen between Ephesians 5 which spoke of marriage as a great foreshadowing or mystery and 1 Corinthians 7 which tells Christians who are preparing for the parousia that it is better not to marry. In the patristic period, one finds a person like Augustine praising the role that marriage plays in the mystery of redemption at the same time his thought is heavily entrenched in the battle of the spirit against the body. Some of his practical comments about marriage were rather harsh. The medieval church was also entrenched in a dualism at the same time it articulated marriage's place among the seven sacraments. It appreciated what the tradition said about the honored place that marriage had in the Christian life. It articulated its importance by emphasizing that the grace or help of God was directly given through a ceremony or sacrament of the church. Given the dynamics of the medieval mind, this approach is understandable.

So also is the Protestant view of marriage understandable within the dynamics of its cultural setting. They had no argument with emphasizing marriage as a great source of God's grace. God was active in the life of the couple and the family. They had an argument with the idea of church that was found so prominent in the medieval period. In the efforts to remove the church as a primary intermediary between the individual and God, the Protestant churches cut down the number of sacraments and played down the importance of those they retained. Even so, the movement still wanted to stress the role of marriage in the plan of God as did the other periods.

The Protestant approach was not any more successful in overcoming the tension between holding the importance of marriage while at the same time affirming the all-encompassing call of God for each individual.

While the Protestant tradition no longer called marriage a sacrament, it remained in most churches an important celebration. While noting the position of the family as a domestic church, the emphasis in most of the tradition was on the individual conversion experience found in the face to face encounter with God. The tension took on different dimensions, but it was not eliminated.

B. The Question of Divorce

After all the arguments were laid to rest, there was in fact little difference in the spirit and practice of marriage in the Catholic and Protestant churches. Both offered very similar views of what a marriage for two people committed to Christ meant. Both saw the life of commitment and love bringing special helps and rewards from God. Both appreciated the special witness that a true Christian marriage brought to the world. Both saw the primary end of marriage to be the procreation of children. Both also saw the value of a church-centered wedding.

The biggest difference came first in the area of regulations. Because the Catholic Church felt that Christian marriage was a special sacrament entrusted to its care, it quite understandably developed an elaborate system of rules and regulations governing the validity and lawfulness of marriage. The Protestants, on the other hand, saw marriage as a natural institution that was part of God's creation. They felt quite content in most cases to allow the civil authorities to regulate the lawfulness and validity of marriage.

An even greater difference, however, can be found in the attitude and practice of divorce. The Catholics, as pointed out earlier, found themselves in a position in which they could not allow divorce. They could not allow divorce even if they wanted to. The sacrament of marriage, in their theology, created a supernatural reality that even the church did not have the authority to change.

The Protestant churches were dealing with a different set of questions. They did not have to confront a special supernatural reality. However, they did have to confront the strong sense of the sacredness of marriage as well as the strong condemnation against divorce found in the New Testament.

There are several passages in the New Testament in which the question of divorce is raised. In each case Jesus clearly upholds the indissolubility of marriage. He forcefully dismisses the Mosaic permission to allow divorce as a concession to the sinfulness of the Jews. He makes it clear that he is calling his followers back to the original ideal. Those who did not wish to live up to this ideal cannot be his followers.

The Protestant authorities, however, did find an argument for allowing divorce in the case of adultery. In the fifth and the nineteenth chapters of Matthew there does seem to be permission for divorce in the case of adultery. All the intricacies of the argument need not be looked at here. However, most churches in the Protestant tradition did allow divorce for significant reasons, particularly for cases of adultery, and did allow remarriage to what it considered the innocent party.

NOTES

1. *The Second Helvetic Confession, 1566* in *The Creeds of Christendom,* Philip Schaff, ed., volume 1 (New York: Harper and Brothers, 1878) p. 411.

2. Ibid., p. 419.

3. Barbara Hargrove, "Family in the White American Protestant Experience," in *Family and Religion*, William V. D'Antonio and Joan Aldous, eds. (Beverly Hills: Sage Publications, 1983) p. 133.

4. Jane Dempsey Douglass, "Women and the Continental Reformation," in *Religion and Sexism*, Rosemary Ruether, ed. (New York: Simon and Schuster, 1974) p. 295.

5. Christopher Hill, *Society and Puritanism in Pre-Revolutionary England* (New York: Schocken Books, 1967) p. 466.

6. Ibid.

7. Kenneth Silverman, *The Life and Times of Cotton Mather* (New York: Harper and Row, Publishers, 1984) p. 57.

8. Hill, pp. 456–58.

9. Ibid., p. 467.

10. Ibid., p. 468.

11. Sang H. Lee, "The Importance of the Family: A Reformed Theological Perspective," in *Faith and Families*, Lindell Sawyers, ed. (Philadelphia: The Geneva Press, 1986) p. 118.

STUDY QUESTIONS

1. Why was the reformation a movement ready to happen?

2. How did the Protestant view of marriage differ from the Catholic?

3. What was the Protestant attitude toward family?

4. What is the tension between realizing the special place of marriage in the Christian life and realizing the unconditional call of individuals in the experience of God?

5. What were the Catholic and Protestant views of divorce?

FURTHER STUDY

Lenski, Gerhard E. *Marriage in the Lutheran Church* (Columbus: The Lutheran Book Concern, 1938). A dated but extensive study of a tradition's view of marriage.

Luther, Martin. *The Estate of Marriage* in *Luther's Works*, volume 45. Walter Brandt, ed. (Philadelphia: Muhlenberg Press, 1962). A look at how marriage is treated in the mentality of the day.

Ruether, Rosemary, ed. *Religion and Sexism* (New York: Simon and Schuster, 1974). A number of excellent essays on numerous periods including the reformation.

Sawyers, Lindell, ed. *Faith and Families* (Philadelphia: The Geneva Press, 1986). Develops the view of family from a number of religious perspectives. Several good essays on the development of marriage in the Protestant tradition.

Stone, Lawrence. *The Past and the Present* (Boston: Routledge and Kegan Paul, 1981). A controversial but interesting history of family.

7.

Marriage in the Modern Period

———————— ◇ ————————

At one level the differences in the theology of marriage between the Catholic and Protestant churches remains the same today. The Catholic Church still insists that marriage is a sacrament. As such it is a pivotal event in the life of the Christian community. The church feels that Christian marriage was made into a special reality by Jesus and as such brings about a cohesion or covenant which cannot be broken by any authority on this earth.

The Protestant churches, on the other hand, continue to insist that marriage is not a special Christian sacrament but a natural institution established by God which brings blessings and helps to those who embrace it. They do generally allow divorce and remarriage not only to what were originally termed innocent parties but to all who show a reasonable promise of living a fruitful Christian commitment.

On another level, however, both traditions have moved far beyond both the medieval and reformation mentalities. The territories they now probe offer promises, challenges, and threats.

A. The Unity of Human Life

The biggest change in the modern Christian church is its rejection of the dualism that anchored the patristic, medieval, and to some extent reformation periods. The decision to take a more holistic view of human nature was not a difficult decision to make. It was, in a sense, a decision that had to be made. The overwhelming conclusion on the part of present culture is that matter and spirit are on a continuum. The importance of environment is undeniable. The importance of physical structure is undeniable. In a sense a person's body is a person's most immediate environment.

Environment is one of those big, all-inclusive, rather nebulous words like culture which no one can define to the satisfaction of ten people hearing the definition. Culture usually refers to the meaning, organizing, and interpretative symbols of life and models of behavior developed by a people with a common experience. Environment includes the realities covered by the idea of culture, but it goes beyond the symbols created by a people to encompass the total convergence of physical and spiritual influences. It is an important word in the history of Christian practice because once the impact of environment became an undeniable reality, the Christian tradition had to recognize that the spiritual and the physical were inseparable. The resulting change in the Christian sense of marriage is dramatic.

The following cases give some indication of how the agenda has shifted:

Case One

Mary McDonald is twenty-seven years old. She comes from a fairly wealthy family. Her mother and father were very intelligent people. Both parents had a weight problem. Her mother had a drinking problem. Both her mother and her father were not very good at expressing their feelings to each other or to those close to them. Despite the fact that they were very active, friendly, and involved in social, religious, and civic causes, they were not close to people. In fact, both felt quite lonely in the midst of plenty. They had plenty of family—six kids and a dog, plenty of people with all their social "friends," and plenty of adventure with at least one good trip a year. Instead of the happiness that is often associated with a full and committed existence, their life was characterized by a strong sense of emptiness. Both parents were treated on and off throughout their adult lives for depression. Neither found a miracle cure.

At one level Mary loves her parents, but she never did like them very much, particularly her mother. She was determined to be a different person. She was not going to let herself swing into those negative moods that characterized her parents' lives. She was not going to be cold and distant as her mother was in the private moments; nor was she going to be a social gadfly running from event to event. She was going to work at being emotionally close to her husband and children.

To date, Mary has shown some but not a great deal of success in her resolve to be different. She is not ready to declare herself an alcoholic. But she does have some heavy drinking periods, and she is about to admit that she cannot be a social drinker. She also fights a weight problem. She controls her eating, but it seems everything she puts to her lips goes to her hips. It would not take much effort for her to get fat.

Her life is better than her parents' in a number of ways. She and her husband are closer. There are periods when her mood swings causes her to be rather distant, but she works at breaking the walls down. She loves her work as a computer analyst and has moved up the ladder very fast, but she feels that she spends good quality time with her children. She avoids getting involved in too many social commitments since her work is so demanding.

Comment: It is as true to say that one can never leave home as it is to say that one can never go home. Given Mary's genetic history, it was probable that she would be intellectually gifted, that she would tend to be overweight, and possibly that she would have a tendency to be an alcoholic and to be depressed. Given her family background, she would probably be an extrovert who sought companionship with many people. It was also probable that she would have a great deal of difficulty being personally and emotionally close to others.

Her life is dependent on her heritage. It is not determined by her past, but her ability to mold her life is limited. However, what she wills can make some difference. What she experiences in her new setting in terms of her husband, children, friends, as well as her surroundings in general will also make a difference.

Case Two

Jim Alvarez is forty-five. Through most of his life he has been a positive person. He has been successful in business. His wife and children in the past have experienced him as a caring, active husband and father. Ever since last year, however, when he lost his parents to a car accident, he has been irritable. He also loses his concentration especially on his job. He shows little patience with his children. He and his wife are now arguing frequently.

Comment: There are times when different circumstances can come into common focus to change a life in a dramatic way. Jim is being hit by the tragic loss of parents who were a significant anchor in his life. This tragedy is probably striking at the same time that he is going through a combination of bodily, social, psychological and economic changes normally lumped under the term mid-life crisis. What he needs is a lot of love and caring from his family and friends to help him through the period. In all likelihood it is a period he can work through if his personal surroundings remain positive. The danger, of course, is that the depression he now feels will simply eat away at the positive life he has built. His life may unwind before he gets his positive rhythm back.

B. A New Perspective on Freedom and Emotions

Neither analysis is important in its detail. What is important is to recognize the modern way of digesting the flow of life. Present thinking sees the human personality as something that simply cannot be tugged from one direction to another, no matter how strong one wills the change. Today human effort and will are respected and admired. However, their success depends in large part on how well human effort works with the total picture. Success generally does not come when a determined individual puts the proverbial head down and charges full speed. Rather success comes when people put their lives in favorable circumstances and then exercise their determination to bring about measured change.

This way of thinking is in stark contrast to the dualism that served as the context for much of Christian thinking in the past. In a world where spirit and matter were seen to be at war, a Christian was called upon to ignore or at least rise above the environment and personal experiences and feelings by a sheer act of the will. A penitential ascribed to the Venerable Bede (d. 735), for example, places a bereaved monk on bread and water "until he can be joyful."[1] For Bede the depression that set in with the death of a loved one was a spiritual blemish. Humans were supposed to exercise the intellect and the will—dimensions associated with the soul—over feelings and emotions which were seen to be expressions of the body. To allow free reign to the emotive part of life would only drag a person down to the dictates of the lower physical appetites.

Humans, in the minds of the medieval people, had to will the positive and the spiritual in life. Monks in particular had to celebrate the entrance into heaven of a victorious Christian even if that Christian happened to be a departing parent. They had to put aside their pangs of separation. Such feelings simply belied how attached one was to this fleeting world.

By contrast, a mourning person today is met with understanding. The common wisdom urges that deeply felt feelings be expressed. Feelings are true. They must be recognized and allowed to work their natural rhythm. Not every mood and every emotion can run rampant, but repression and denial do not contribute to a positive life. If a bereaved person does not deal with the feelings of separation and hurt, these human realities—according to the modern view—will develop into scars that will bleed at certain points of stress. The conscious ignores the subconscious only at its own peril. There is no question of mind over body. The spirit pulses from the body and must recognize its physical demands as heralding basic human needs.

C. Sources of Change

Modern culture did not arrive at this close tie between the physical and the spiritual in any leisurely fashion. Its conclusions are first the result of an ever-increasing positive experience of the world, particularly in western culture which has been the dominant setting for Christian theology up until recent times. If daily domestic life provides the majority of people with a comfortable and secure experience, it is rather difficult to spurn the beauty and goodness of this world. If by contrast life on this earth is short and unstable, if it demands that one scratch the ground eighteen hours a day just to exist, then it is easy to look for some afterlife in which the miseries of the world can be escaped.

But this common positive experience of the world has also been accompanied by developments in the physical and social sciences. Persistent human investigation has led to sophisticated methods for stepping back and observing how the physical and the personal interact. The evidence of the older sciences such as medicine and physics continually indicated that spirit and matter were intertwined. Newer fields of social study that have developed in earnest in the twentieth century such as psychology and sociology simply confirmed the mounting evidence of the harder sciences.

The scientific method is not new, of course, but its conclusions of the last hundred years have been dramatic. Darwin proposed his theory of survival of the fittest only a little over a hundred years ago. He was met with cries of derision by many educated people. Freud offered his theories of psychoanalysis at the turn of the century. He was hooted from the podium. Both today, though, have been accepted and significantly corrected. Their underlying presumptions, however, grew out of the growing consensus of the day.

Sociology has led people to realize how much a person owes to the social, economic, and personal surroundings. There are cases in which a person rises above the surroundings, but the exception simply affirms the rule.

Psychology is filled with lesson after lesson of how the experiences of the child shape and form the adult. It also works with biology to confirm that the aging body has much to do with the changing spirit of the person. Biology on its own explains much about the human make-up. The person with Down's syndrome would be entirely different than if the extra chromosome had not developed in the fertilized egg. The conclusion is overwhelming. Physical structure sets the parameters of reality.

Soybeans, petroleum, and other products can be reconstructed into plastics from which everything from sandwich bags to space age helmets is made. In turn human persons can be changed in a fundamental way by raising or lowering the acid content of the body, by altering the brain through chemicals or surgery, or by altering the genetic heritage.

The question is: What does all this have to do with the issue at hand? What does all this have to do with the Christian sense and practice of marriage? The answer is quite simple and direct. Once spiritual growth and physical change were seen as complementary, the community significantly shifted its thinking about the place of marriage in the Christian vocation.

Once the connection was made between spirit and matter, marriage was raised to a new status. Marriage was once again placed on a pedestal as it was in the Old Testament although for very different reasons. The parousia or the second coming was no longer expected within the immediate lifetime of the community. Marriage, therefore, was no longer seen as a distraction. Dualism was now ruled out. Somehow the search for God had to reconcile itself with the material world in general and marriage in particular.

D. Two Basic Approaches

In looking at the literature of churches today, there are two fundamental ways of picturing the importance of the family and marriage. First, the family is seen as the basic human community which prepares its members for their search for God. The marital relationship within the family is seen as fundamental to the development of the partners. The second approach sees the family as providing a more direct link to God.

The first approach can be seen in a statement issued by a body in the United Methodist Church:

> Specifically, the church is concerned that families provide a growing experience in understanding God and the world and in demonstrating the reality of God's love in the world. God's love, expressed in families

through affectional and emotional ties and commitment to responsible relationships, as well as providing the necessities of life, is essential for personal stability and personality growth.[2]

In the Methodist statement the connection between God and the family is tentative. It provides the "experience in understanding God." There is also some connection between God's love and family life expressed "through affectional and emotional ties and commitment." In short the family is seen as an environment that prepares one to realize the activity and nature of God. There does not seem to be any attempt at developing a direct equation between the experience of family and the experience of God.

The second approach, suggested in the previous chapter on the New Testament, presents a more direct link. When Paul in the New Testament spoke of the marital relationship, he saw marriage as distracting the Christian. He advised the husband and wife to separate for a short time so that they could pray. He advised this temporary separation only if both parties mutually agreed to do so. The message was obvious, however. Marriage was seen as a distraction.

In this work's initial treatment of the New Testament the diagram below was offered to show the significant contrast between the thinking in the period of the gospels and epistles and this second way of thinking present in the modern period.

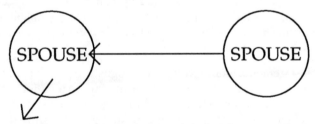

God found in the true depths of daily life, especially in the true depths of a loved one.

This second view is found more readily in Catholic writings than in Protestant literature. Historically, the Catholic tradition has had an easier time accepting the compatibility of creation and God. Its doctrine of redemption and original sin saw creation restored more clearly to the graces of God. Therefore, it has an easier time speaking of the compatibility of this world with the life of God. It does not drop all cautions, however, because it wishes to maintain the transcendence of God. In other words, God is infinite and never can be fully contained in any experience of this world.

With that limitation set, however, the underlying imagery of this second approach sees God at the heart of all creation. If a person probes the world deeply enough, one finds God. God is seen as the ground of all being. A shallow or blind approach to the goods of the world can cause one to stop at the surface. The result is a shallow life that fails to capture the true mystery and beauty of reality. However, if one learns to go beyond the surface of the world, one finds the true meaning or ground even if the name God is not used. In more optimistic terms, creation can be seen as God-soaked.

When applied specifically to marriage, church statements incorporating this more direct link between marriage and the search for God offer statements such as the following one of Pope Paul VI:

> There is no married love which in its deepest joy is not an impetus toward the infinite and does not by reason of its very dynamism aim to be total, faithful, exclusive and fruitful.[3]

In more forceful language one finds the national catechism for adults sanctioned by the Dutch bishops making the following statement:

> To say that the erotic is good would be inadequate. We use "erotic" here for sexuality in all its facets—physical, psychic, etc. It is a marvelous and creative force in us. . . . It is only when integrated in the totality of man's being that we can see how good and lovely the erotic is. Everyone knows how dear the beloved is to the lover. The attractiveness of another is seen and activated. Something of the infinite shines through the beloved, something to which one is drawn to give oneself totally.[4]

Such statements would truly make Augustine turn over in his grave. Gone is the sense that any physical pleasure, not to mention venereal or carnal indulgence, is automatically a hindrance for the soul in its search for God. Gone also is the fear for the lurking disorder known as concupiscence. The appetites and bodily drives are no longer seen as disorders that try to overwhelm the person trying to introduce discipline and control into life. The challenge of human life is not seen as an attempt to weed out imperfections. Rather, the task is to expand the human spirit by using the appetites and drives as so much fuel to drive the person beyond a self-centered life.

E. Self-Centeredness, Marriage, and the Search for God

Self-centeredness is now seen as the key sin. Loneliness, boredom, love, and sexual desire are the engines which drive the person to seek fresher relationships that allow the individual to live beyond the self. It is the hunger for creativity that constantly goads an individual. There is something planted in the human which does not allow it to remain comfortably isolated within itself. Each person has a restlessness that urges newer, deeper relationships with others or the Other.

Certainly the Christian view of marriage and family must be changed with such a significant shift in the underlying images. The shift is evident in the statements quoted above. However, the statements are not unequivocal in their equation of family and God. Marriage and family are important, in some statements normally indispensable, in the search for God. However, there is not in either approach a simple equation between the domestic experience and the experience of God.

In Paul VI's statement it is only in the "deepest joy" of the marital relationship that one finds "an impetus toward the infinite." In the national catechism only "something of the infinite shines through the beloved." In other words neither statement wants to domesticate God. Neither wishes to dismiss the transcendent element of God whose presence is so awesome that it has filled many with fear and trembling.

There is a danger in the humanism of the day to turn God into a warm puppy. The church statements want to acknowledge the immanent presence of God. They do not want to ignore the awesomeness of God that has overwhelmed people through the centuries. While the statements clearly emphasize the loving God that can be known in a loving home, both approaches see the connection as an imperfect one. The experiences of life are limited, and the nature of God is infinite.

F. The Family as Central

There are differences in emphasis within the different Christian traditions and even within the same tradition in the way the family is treated. Overall, however, there is general unanimity on the central importance of family. The family is paramount for the normal pattern of Christian life today. The American Baptists, for example, found that as their Statements of Concern Committee solicited issues from around the country, "again and again the family was number one in . . . concern."[5] The 183rd General Assembly of the United Presbyterian Church "designated family life as one of the more urgent concerns. . . ."[6] The United Methodists claim that "whatever in society threatens families threatens the church. . . ."[7] The Lutheran Church in America states: "There is no greater challenge today than in the family, for it is intended by God to be that basic community in which personhood is fostered."[8] John Paul II asserts "the family as the first and vital cell of society."[9]

This acceptance of the family as the basic unit not only of society but also of the church clearly reflects the environmental view that characterizes present culture. The family is the place where everything starts. If one realizes the formative influence of the environment, then there can be no talk about pursuing a Christian life that ignores where everything begins.

The family is seen as the place where one learns the basics of humanity. As the Second Vatican Council expresses rather movingly, "the family is a kind of school of deeper humanity."[10] It is the place where one learns how to love and be loved—an experience so essential for human identity:

> Man cannot live without love. He remains a being that is incomprehensible for himself; his life is senseless, if love is not revealed to him, if he does not encounter love, if he does not experience it and make it his own, if he does not participate intimately in it.[11]

Coming from the Christian perspective, of course, that identity is usually seen as being closely tied with realizing one's religious roots. The United Methodists state: "In the beginning God created family. Through this gracious gift we all enter into life, find our identity, claim our heritage, and seek our mission as God's children."[12] The Lutheran Church–Missouri Synod states in one publication that "family life is an opportunity for individual family members to live out the love and forgiveness which is theirs in Jesus Christ."[13]

Some statements start from a simple biblical observation: "Mother, father and children are gifts of God. God made Adam and Eve to give Him glory as the crown of his creation and to continue His creation as parents of children. . . ."[14] Others take a more philosophical approach:

> Willed by God in the very act of creation, marriage and the family are interiorly ordained to fulfillment in Christ and have need of his graces in order to be healed from the wounds of sin and restored to their "beginning," that is, to full understanding and the full realization of God's plan.[15]

Marriage and the family, then, are placed in the center of Christian living.

G. The Specific Purpose of Marriage

If the basic view of the human challenge has shifted as the previous paragraphs have suggested, then it would be reasonable to expect a significant shift in the church's thinking about the end or goal of marriage. Such indeed is the case.

In the Old Testament marriage was seen as the way to achieve immortality, security, prosperity, and identity. In the New Testament, marriage was seen as a distraction from the imminent second coming which would establish a radical new order on this earth. It was seen as the wisest choice for those who could not control the appetites of this life. In a sense, then, marriage was seen as a way of expressing one's passions within a responsible lifestyle. Because the second coming was to establish a new order, there was not a stress on the need for continuing the species.

The dualism which set in with the early centuries of the church went one step further. It could not champion the expression of human passions in any form even within the loving commitment of marriage. In that sense the church after the second century rejected the view of the New Testament. As the hoped for new order failed to develop, however, the church faced a new reality. The species must continue to produce by normal ways. The conclusion was easy. Marriage was declared good by scripture. The species must continue. Therefore, marriage must be good primarily because it continued the species. This essential task was the main reason for the institution of marriage.

There were other goods associated with marriage, particularly by Augustine. There was the committed love between the spouses. There was the unique love between parent and child. There was the witness the Christian family could give to non-Christians. But the only reason for exercising the marital act was to have children. Any deliberate enjoyment of the carnal pleasures during intercourse was prohibited.

The medieval period worked primarily within the confines of the tradition it inherited. However, as the decades passed, the church eventually worked its way back to the New Testament position of also seeing marriage as a cure for concupiscence. It helped the two partners to remain faithful to each other.

With the reformation period, one finds in both the Protestant and Catholic traditions a growing appreciation of the interpersonal value of marriage. Marriage was seen as a way of helping two people grow in love. Their physical intimacy is gradually seen as a help in bonding the love and commitment expressed to each other. But the primary end of the institution of marriage is still presented as the procreation of children. Marriage is the institution set up by God to multiply the species. According to this thinking, there would be no reason to marry if one did not want children. The friendship and help between the spouses could be experienced outside of marriage. It was not within the parameters of the day to think of having intercourse without intending to have children.

Looking at this schema, then, there are significant shifts within the Christian tradition, particularly between the Old Testament and the New Testament, between the New Testament and the patristic period, and between the medieval and the reformation period. The difference between the present appreciation of marriage and that of previous periods can be seen in a statement about birth control by the Lambeth Conference in the 1930s. This is an international meeting of the churches who belong to the Anglican body. It meets every few years to address the concerns of the tradition. The statement issued by the conference in the 1930s was the first one by a mainstream church to accept the practice of artificial birth control:

> Where there is a clearly felt moral obligation to limit or avoid parenthood, the method must be decided on Christian principles. The primary and obvious method is complete abstinence from intercourse (as far as may be necessary) in a life of discipline and self-control lived in the power of the Holy Spirit. Nevertheless, in those cases where there is such a clearly felt moral obligation to limit or avoid parenthood, and where there is a morally sound reason for avoiding complete abstinence, the Conference agrees that other methods may be used, provided that this is done in the light of the same Christian principles. The Conference records its strong condemnation of the use of any methods of conception-control from motives of selfishness, luxury or mere convenience.[16]

The wording of this statement shows just how much the churches have changed in just over fifty years, not only in their thinking about birth control but in their thinking about marriage in general. It speaks of "a clearly felt moral obligation to limit . . . parenthood." The married couple, in other words, would normally be expected to have children if possible. Simply avoiding children because of personal choice or career demands is not even given adequate stage. Implicitly, marriage is an institution which is specifically designed to continue the race.

The statement argues that the "primary and obvious method is complete abstinence from intercourse . . . in a life of discipline and self-control." The call for complete abstinence is significant in its own right. Implied in the statement, however, is a failure to appreciate the beauty of physical intimacy. At no point does the statement pause to acknowledge the efficacy of physical intimacy for the two trying to grow in their love and support of each other.

To some extent the statement must be taken in its context. It is a politically designed work meant to garner as many votes as possible in a convention that had turned down similar proposals favoring birth control in previous years. The writers did not worry about those members of the conference who had an appreciation of physical intimacy as a legitimate end in itself. Their vote was assured. To that extent the statement is tilted to the traditionalist, dualistic side. Still, the fact that the conference had to make such concessions to a dualistic approach to life is a testimony to how entrenched that way of thinking still was in the church.

By contrast the Christian churches today have clearly moved from seeing marriage primarily as an institution for procreation. Certainly, they do not play down the importance of children. They do, however, see the growth in love and commitment between the partners as an equally significant purpose in marriage. As the earlier statements indicated, the churches today generally appreciate the importance of the physical in achieving this intimacy.

In the Episcopal Church, for example, which belongs to the Anglican body, there is a statement which couples seeking to be married are asked to sign stating their belief in marriage:

> We believe it is for the purpose of mutual fellowship, encouragement, and understanding, for the procreation . . . of children, and their physical and spiritual nurture, and for the safeguarding and benefit of society. . . .[17]

The statement tries to call the couple beyond their own mutual world to a greater appreciation of the value of children and the importance of family for the well-being of society. However, it does see marriage as a means of growing together in love.

Moving the growth of the couple on par with the desire to have children is the rule in the Christian churches. They also frequently emphasize the importance of the physical in reaching for each other. A working draft of the American Lutheran Church entitled, "Teachings and Practice on Marriage and Divorce," for example, states, "Sexual differences are of God's good design, intended to bring joy and enrichment to human life as well as to provide for procreation."[18]

Unlike its predecessors, then, there is a comfortableness in the modern church with physical intimacy. The mutual enjoyment of physical pleasure is not seen as giving in to the lower appetites. It is not seen as bowing to the lower physical world. On the contrary, within the commitment of marriage, physical intimacy is now seen as expressing the deepest levels of one's being. It is seen as a life-giving way of reaching for the other. It is a way of stimulating the limited love achieved in the reality of a marriage. It is a way of repairing the hurts and the distances that continually frustrate two people who want to be close to each other.

Physical intimacy in marriage, then, is appreciated for the support it offers the couple who are reaching for the personal relationship. However, the personal relationship itself is seen as paramount in importance for the meaning of Christian marriage. The love between the husband and wife is no longer seen as a distraction. It is no longer seen as a secondary good. It is seen as a primary purpose in a marriage. Without it the couple and the children will have a very difficult time finding God.

Marriage, of course, is still seen as a way of continuing the race. Children are important in marriage. In general the traditions see children as the natural fruit of a loving commitment. Many statements see children as a true way of calling the couple beyond themselves into a richer life. Some of the Christian traditions, particularly the Catholic, would insist that all acts of intercourse be open to conception. At least the couple is discouraged from using artificial means of birth control and at marriage they must acknowledge that they have not ruled out having children. But the modern traditions do not speak of children as the primary end in marriage with the personal relationship assigned to secondary importance.

H. Specific Questions

The Christian churches are obviously in tension with the larger culture on many points. On issues specifically relevant to marriage, the church feels called to witness to the importance of lifelong commitments. Present society is marked by its fluidity. When something does not work or works only imperfectly, the first impulse is to buy or make something new.

The Question of Divorce

People today are committed. The sense of resolve in the face of mounting difficulties, however, is weakened in the society taken as a whole. The church in turn feels compelled to witness to its heritage. It must celebrate the life that comes with a depth of commitment.

There are times when problems cause an irreparable rift in the married life. All churches provide for some type of divorce or separation. Some, such as the Catholic Church, do not allow for remarriage. However, there is in the literature of most of the churches a constant encouragement for their members to work out problems where possible. In addition to this general community support, many churches try to develop counseling programs to help in particular situations. There is a constant voice that appreciates the virtues of stability in family life. It is not a stability at any cost. But commitment and stability are recognized virtues.

The Value of Sexual Expression

The churches also warn against the recreational view of sex. The pleasures of this world are not to be enjoyed as so many offerings in the feast of life. A consumerism present in society encourages a person to get as much as possible. It develops a quantitative posture toward the consumption of pleasure. The Christian tradition warns, however, that the secret of life lies in the depth of relationship.

Sexual relations, in the Christian view, find true fulfillment in a bonding that involves all the dimensions of one's being. Sexual pleasure is one of the energies that propels a person out of the self. People are in a sense driven to strive for the difficult gift of bonding with another. Recreational sex often makes such an encompassing relationship either difficult or impossible. It frequently causes distrust and jealousy in a life aimed at pleasing the self in a direct and immediate way.

But the churches do not simply serve as a correction to the culture. They have learned much from the experience of modern society. On the most rudimentary level, the skills of history and languages have allowed the Christian community to look back on its own history and to appreciate its own change. The community realizes that it has developed. It also realizes that it has not developed in a vacuum. It has adjusted to other peoples in ways which have not always done it proud. It must also guard against adjusting to the present culture in ways that would not be faithful to its establishing vision.

On a more positive note, however, the faith community has learned from the modern culture how to appreciate the physical world. It has also learned how to celebrate the interpersonal and the relational. From one perspective, both the things of this world and the people of this world are effective vehicles for discovering God and the holy. From another perspective God and the sacred are ways of appreciating the world.

The Scriptural Guideposts

From the point of view of the scriptural guideposts used in this chapter, the modern era readily embraces some points and struggles with others. Scripture warns that all have faults and will stumble in a significant way. On one level, the modern humanistic society comfortably accepts human frailty. Alcoholics or other chemically dependent people are not dismissed as evil. They are seen as people with an illness that can be controlled. Similarly, people who have a moral lapse of one bent or another are generally allowed to put their past behind them. Failures and flaws do not rule out greatness.

George Washington had wooden false teeth, was not well versed in military strategy, and due at least in part to personal limitations had a weak second term as president. Yet his importance to both the Revolutionary War and the early political life of the republic is genuinely appreciated. Lincoln was not the simple backwoodsman that his myth suggested. He also had severe bouts of depression and self-doubt, and he condoned some questionable efforts to cover for a wife who had her personal tortures. He is still placed at the top of most people's list of presidents.

Amidst this modern ability to balance limitations and greatness, however, there is still the desire to create gods. There are Vince Lombardi, Mother Teresa, and even Ronald Reagan. For some, these people can do or did not do any wrong. They are enshrined. In other words we are inconsistent as a people. Most testimonial dinners demonstrate our need to make gods and goddesses. The lusty sales of scandal tabloids, however, illustrate the thrill people experience at the fall of the exalted.

This vacillation between balance, worship, and cynicism has its expression in the present view of family. One has but to look at television to find that Roseanne has replaced Donna Reed; Theo Huxtable, Bud Anderson; and the Golden Girls, Miss Brooks. There is a greater tendency to see the characters in a more realistic way. Modern casts are filled with people with obvious passions, faults, and inconsistencies.

Still the sense of romantic love does not die easily. We still want to see the perfect couple who remain passionately taken with each other both physically and personally even after a household filled with kids. There may not be room for Ozzie and Harriet, but there is still an appetite for the Keatons and the Huxtables.

The romantic vision of marriage, if not put into some perspective, can be harmful. There is not a time in a marriage when the phrase "for better and for worse" does not constantly echo through the relationship. The tradition's counsel to accept the limited and the flawed is a needed voice to balance the dominance of romantic love that is present in at least one level of the society.

The tradition balances this caution, however, with its own reminder that all are made in the image and likeness of God. Despite the failures, in other words, all are called to a life of discipleship. All are called to a greatness as they respond to the spark of God contained in each person.

At times the churches, in their effort to faithfully witness to this call, find themselves in the same circumstances that the vision of romantic love creates. At times church statements get too idealistic. They speak about living life in the image of God; they speak of the infinite shining through the marital relationship; they speak of the unsurpassable joys of married life. Many a couple are left simply shaking their heads. Myrtle has to turn to Matt and wonder what went wrong with their life.

In other words, statements that get too idealistic fail to celebrate the muted good that is achieved in the day to day relationships of families that—as the first scriptural point emphasized—will experience noted flaws. Language that is idealistic can call people beyond their present achievements. Language that is too idealistic can mock the measured achievements that characterize any marriage and family.

In addressing the third scriptural point—the special quality of Christian marriage—it is easy to see how the churches are almost forced to stress what is unique about the Christian sense of marriage. The culture faces such a turmoil in terms of stability in family life that the churches struggle with the issue in clear and explicit terms.

Finally, the role of the family in the mission of the church is appreciated today in ways far surpassing previous cultures. More specifics will be mentioned later in this book. Suffice it to say that once family was appreciated as the fundamental human environment, its challenge in bringing into reality the kingdom of God on earth was obvious.

CONCLUSION

The Christian tradition has obviously gone through many twists and turns on its journey through the different rhythms of western civilization. The tradition has served it well at certain points as it resisted some peculiarities of the culture. At times it has resisted the culture when it should not have. It mistook a desire for safety in the familiar as an essential ingredient of its founding revelation. When the church opened itself to the insights of the culture, in some ways it found they simply enriched the tradition.

As challenging as the tradition has been to this point, the road ahead promises to be as adventurous. To date the awareness of the church has been dominated by western ways. Today, however, the largest growth in church membership has been in third world countries. This increase combined with a greater sensitivity to the global community will certainly push the church to expand its boundaries in new ways. Marriage and family traditions in Nigeria, in Peru, and in Vietnam are significantly different from those found in western Europe.

Notes

1. John T. McNeill, *A History of the Cure of Souls* (New York: Harper and Row, 1951) p. 120.

2. Family Life Committee: The United Methodist Church, *Family Life: A Resolution* (Nashville: Discipleship Resources, 1980) p. 6.

3. Paul VI, "Address to the International Meeting of the Teams of Our Lady" (May 4, 1970), quoted in *A Vision and Strategy* (Washington: United States Catholic Conference, 1978) p. 30.

4. *A New Catechism* (New York: Herder and Herder, 1967) p. 384.

5. "The Family—A Christian Concern," National Ministries: American Baptist Churches (Valley Forge, 1979).

6. *Minutes of the General Assembly of the United Presbyterian Church in the United States of America*, Part I, One Hundred and Eighty-Third General Assembly, 1971 (New York: Office of the General Assembly) p. 169.

7. United Methodist Church, p. 1.

8. "Sex, Marriage, and Family," *Social Statement of the Lutheran Church in America* (New York: Board of Social Ministry) p. 2.

9. John Paul II, *On the Family* (Washington: United States Catholic Conference, 1981) p. 41.

10. "Pastoral Constitution on the Church in the Modern World," section 52, *Documents of Vatican II*, William M. Abbott, ed. (New York: America Press, 1966) p. 257.

11. John Paul II, p. 16.

12. United Methodist Church, p. 1.

13. Ronald W. Brusius, *Family Life Education*, Information Bulletin 70080: Board of Parish Education (St. Louis: The Lutheran Church-Missouri Synod) p. 3.

14. Ronald W. Brusius, *Family Enrichment in Your Congregation*, Information Bulletin 70480: Board of Parish Education (St. Louis: The Lutheran Church-Missouri Synod) p. 1.

15. John Paul II, p. 2.

16. Quoted in Anthony Kosnik, et al., *Human Sexuality* (New York: Paulist Press, 1979) p. 45.

17. Marriage Canons in *Church and Society: Social Policy of the Episcopal Church* (New York: Episcopal Church Center) p. 330.

18. Standing Committee for the Office of Church in Society, "Teachings and Practice on Marriage and Divorce" (Minneapolis: The American Lutheran Church, 1981) p. 1.

STUDY QUESTIONS

1. Explain why the modern Christian church rejects dualism.

2. Why has the Christian view of marriage changed since the physical and the spiritual are seen on a continuum?

3. According to modern church thinking, how does the family help in the search for God?

4. According to present Christian thinking, what is the purpose and the aim of marriage?

5. How does the Christian tradition challenge as well as learn from the modern culture?

FURTHER STUDY

Cooke, Bernard J. *Sacraments and Sacramentality* (Mystic, Connecticut: Twenty-Third Publications, 1983). A study of a modern approach to sacraments that uses marriage as a starting point.

D'Antonio, William V. and Joan Aldous, eds. *Family and Religion* (Beverly Hills: Sage Publications, 1983). Series of essays reflecting modern scholarship in the social sciences.

McDannell, Colleen. *The Christian Home in Victorian America, 1840–1900* (Bloomington: Indiana University Press, 1986). Good treatment of a given period which combines domestic practice with theory.

Mackin, Theodore. *The Marital Sacrament* (New York: Paulist Press, 1989). Studies the modern period in the context of a larger historical work.

———— *What Is Marriage?* (New York: Paulist Press, 1982). A history of the theology of marriage in the Catholic Church.

8.

The Christian Perspective's Challenge for Marriage

——————— ◇ ———————

Scene: A hot July night in the bedroom of Gene and Patty Snyder. A storm must be brewing because the wind has picked up. Both feel excited as the air pushes aside the curtains and moves across their damp, clammy bodies that were almost sweating. The couple, when they first retired, felt a need for each other that night but were discouraged by the energy-sapping heat. Now stirred by the dance of the air, he begins to run his hand along her leg. He cups her ankle, rubs his finger along her retrieving instep, and finally moves up to play with her clustered varicose veins just behind her left knee.

Patty: "You animal," she responded playfully. She rolled over and lightly grabbed his double chin in her teeth.

Gene: "Don't be gross, Patty," he said with little determination. Her playfulness only heightened his desire. The feeling of lust was reassuring to him. At forty-two the fire sometimes is not there. Its periodic absence scares him. A few years ago almost anything could get the juices flowing. Lately, however, his desire was not always predictable. This slightly plump woman who was about to join him in the fifth decade of life still had a feistiness and bounce to her which could draw him and excite him.

"Hey! Cut that out. You are going to give me one enormous hickey! What are they going to think at the office? What are they going to think at the breakfast table tomorrow? Need I remind you that teenagers notice things, especially things like that?"

Patty: "I'm sorry. It's just that I used to like to play with your hair when we wrestled. That's gone now. I find the chin which you added just as much fun," she said with a giggle. As the words flowed, though, her body tensed ever so much. She had to be careful with him.

She realized how sensitive he had become about his aging. She also sensed that his desire for her was not as strong. She kept telling herself that it was not a loss of interest in her. She knew it was not uncommon for men his age to have lapses in interest. She also remembered the first time he could not respond to her. They were both pretty shook.

It had been difficult for her though. She had had so many strange feelings. Her body was going through so many changes. She needed to be held and wanted. When he could not respond, she thought of some wild things including the possibility that he was having an affair.

Gene: "God, you feel so good to me," he said as he moved his fingers up her leg. There was something about moments such as this when he realized what a blessing it was to have a person who could be there through the hair loss, the extra twenty-five soft pounds, the career disappointments, the death of the parents, and the simple boredom of life. In a world where things that do not look good or work well are quickly dumped, it is a blessing to have each other. Having each other helped them realize that there is a depth and a fabric to life. To have each other helped them make it through the roughest spots. When Patty found that she was pregnant two years ago, they thought about abortion. She made such a thing of burning the diapers and crib when Jeff, their third child, became potty trained and crib free. Pregnancy at thirty-eight was not planned. They saw each other through the shock and disruption of their life. They got on each other's nerves as they thought about abortion and as they worked their way through two months of colic crying. They leaned on each other, though, and made it.

Patty: "You still dance and move pretty well," she said. The heat and dampness of the evening lubricated any part of their bodies that touched. There were times in their life when she did not like this man. She was always able to work her way through those feelings, though, and discover his basic decency. Each time she discovered his value, her own worth grew ever so much.

They moved in rhythm. The sense that this woman who had so much poise and worth would abandon her self-possession so completely with him brought him to climax sooner than he wanted. She found a pimple on the top of his head. At the moment she finally came to her orgasm, she popped the pimple to a quick grunt of his pain.

Gene: "God, you are gross," he murmured as they settled into each other's arms.

They lay there for about ten minutes. The seventeen year old came in an hour late at 1:00 AM and woke the baby when he tripped over the box in the hall. At least they both hoped that was the reason why he stumbled and fell.

Patty: "Let's reverse stereotypes. You get the baby, and I will go dialogue with the eldest son."

◇

Americans marry for a rather strange reason. They marry for love or intimacy. They are seeking to be close to another person. That, at least, is the conscious intention behind the search for a spouse. In fact, there is a whole spectrum of reasons why people today seek to bond with another. We want security. We want predictability and stability. We want roots or belonging. We wish to live on through possible offspring. We are seeking influence or social position.

These "old-fashioned" reasons for establishing a family are not in the forefront of a person's mind in looking for marriage. They are not completely absent, however, even though their role in most marriages has faded to the background. Indeed, the primary conscious reason for marriage in our society is that the prospective spouses want love. Even more to the point, they want the form of love which allows them to be close to one another.

But why is this love, this intimacy, such a strange reason for marriage? What other reason would there be for getting married? You meet someone. You fall in love. You get married and usually have children. That is the plan for most people today. That has been the plan since the start of civilization as we know it. There have been variations of the central plan. There have not been major departures from it.

Wrong. As the previous chapters have indicated, the traditional family in the west has existed primarily for social, economic, educational, and security reasons. Obviously, love of some variety and perhaps even intimacy often developed once the marriage took place. Just as obvious, often it did not. It is very difficult to get a perspective on what roles these words love and intimacy have played in the family throughout western history. It is even very difficult determining what role they play in marriage today. In a sense love is something that can be found in television, movies, or a Harlequin romance. It can also be found in a couple who have known each other for no more than a few weeks. After any length of time, the simple reality of intimate love quickly mutates into some very strange forms. To capture the reality of love, one needs many shades of love—at least as many shades as Sherman-Williams carries on its color charts.

Somewhere along the line, however, intimacy or love, perhaps their muted form companionship, became the primary reason for marriage. The importance of personal bonding in marriage rose in direct proportion as the other functions of the family were absorbed by different institutions in society. The family was no longer the place where one learned the professional trade. Family members no longer worked on the family farm or in the family craft. Eventually a member had to leave the domestic unit to be educated in specialized centers called schools. Today the young college graduates take their individual talents and move to San Diego or Dallas from Allentown, Pennsylvania, and Utica, New York, to work in the job that offers the best market price. Similarly, if sickness or old age takes its toll on a family member, chicken soup and the hot water bottle from the array of home remedies are quickly dismissed in favor of the doctor's office, the outpatient clinic, or the probing machines and needles of the hospital stay.

The individual is well cared for in our society, but many individuals feel a need to belong. People want to bond, want to be needed for themselves and not for what they can do. The family of origin can fulfill these needs to some extent, but the adults are expected to "live on their own." Thanksgiving, Christmas, Easter, periodic birthdays and anniversaries, and weekend cookouts are not enough belonging and contact for the average adult. Most need a more immediate community. That is why a contemporary couple marry and usually have children.

In a sense, personal love is probably needed more today than in the traditional family. As the passages from the Albigensian struggle in an earlier chapter indicated, there was a bonding present in the more traditional society as the family served most of the basic functions needed by both the individual and the society. There was not always a great deal of personal affection present. In a sense the lack of personal affection was less threatening to the traditional family since the bonding came from a more corporate sense of identity that contrasts sharply to the individualism of today.

How, then, does the present marriage based on human affection compare to the more traditional family? Certainly it is more fragile. Certainly it can bring a greater intensity to life.

A. The Search for Intimacy

Everyone assumes that all people want intimacy. Our modern society is built on interpersonal relationships. Who does not want to be close to another person? Surprising as the answer might seem, quite a few people do not want to be intimate. At least they lack the personal qualities or personal drive to be open and trusting enough to achieve the intimacy that appears so attractive to everyone. People want the end product seen in the loving affection of a romantic picture. Intimacy, however, does not come easy. Many are incapable or unwilling to make the necessary journey.

Seldom do couples go into a marriage with a good sense of the other's personal needs. Most of the time a prospective spouse cannot discuss what the other's sense of intimacy is because few men or women are aware of their own expectations and limitations. A case in point would be in order:

Buffy and Biff married last October. Biff has had one year of experience in a local accounting firm. Buffy was one year behind him in school and just recently graduated. She is looking for a teaching job in English. He finds her exciting. She looks great. She smells great. His spirits and his body come alive when she is around. He likes her softness, her ease in relating with people, her infectious giggle, her sense of adventure as she never settles for the apparent or the ordinary.

Buffy on the other hand loves his hardness, his strength, his security, his sense of control. He can take stock of a situation, step back and calculate, and come to a reasonable conclusion as to how the situation should be handled. If things get hairy, he can usually put the pieces back together.

When they were together before marriage, they loved each other's company. They would rather be together than with any other people. After a half dozen months of marriage, however, there is trouble in paradise.

Buffy grew up in settings where she could always share her feelings with the people around her. In her younger years there was always her mother. Later, as a teen, when her mother had to be protected from the realities of life or at least the realities of Buffy's life, she had her girl friends. Finally, in college there was always a running conversation in which others were talking about how they felt. When she looks back on the constant chatter in the sorority house, it probably centered more on feelings than on sex or school or money. She is aware of her strong mood swings. She can be very high, and she can also hit bottom. At either of those extremes she has a real need to talk her way through and to share her feelings with others.

Biff on the other hand is what could be termed a man of few words. His father did not talk a lot. His uncles did not talk a lot. Robert Redford, Clint Eastwood, Burt Reynolds, his high school coach Cyril Beorokoski, Sylvester Stallone, and more recently Rob Lowe and Tom Cruise did not talk a lot. His high school friend Pete Puma, his college roommate Percy Jackson, his fraternity brothers—they did talk quite a bit. They did not spend a great deal of time talking about their emotions, however. Rather, their world of conversation was dominated by sports, girls, sex, school, religion, politics, and most certainly parties. They talked about things going on much more than their reactions to things going on or their mood swings. When feelings were expressed, they were mentioned in a direct fashion and not belabored.

Buffy and Biff were brought up in two different worlds. As they face life together, they must not only adjust to each other. They must also become aware of how they are different. They must learn to know themselves better.

Obviously, the new husband and wife have difficulty in meeting each other's needs. There are friends, and there are jobs. More often than not, however, their personal time when they can let their guards down and unwind is spent in the presence of each other. She tires him out. He infuriates her because he will not tell her what is going on inside of him.

In a sense the very thing that attracted them to each other—their differences—are now causing problems as they reach out to each other. On one level it could be argued that they have a different need for intimacy. At another, probably a more accurate level, it could be argued that they achieve intimacy in different ways. She depends heavily on talking about what is inside her. He is satisfied in sharing actions, in the camaraderie that comes with sharing a common task.

Why did Biff and Buffy fail to discuss their different ways of finding closeness with others? The most obvious answer is that they were not aware of their needs or the way they related with others. Even if they took Psychology 101 and had some sense of their ways of relating, who could discuss such heavy things as communication when they are in love?

The search for intimacy is a maddening quest. Martin Buber seemed to have given many people some helpful handles when he spoke of "I-Thou," "I-You," and "I-It" relationships.[1]

The first phrase (I-Thou) captures the moments of intense intimacy. At such times there is a real rubbing of souls. The presence of the other is dramatic and moving. The closeness, the immediacy makes the blood run quicker in rhythm with the heart. Even the sinuses clear up, and the headache fades if the moment lasts long enough. The trouble is that such experiences of intensity are so demanding, so fatiguing, so fragile that they seldom last long. Like olfactory fatigue, the senses and the self simply cannot maintain that level of awareness. It climaxes. It fades.

The thrill of the experience remains and is enjoyed in an individual's memory and fantasy life. The quest for renewed experiences is often frustrating, however. John Cheever captures the maddening dance in one of his short stories, "The Sorrows of Gin." Amy, a fourth grader, is receiving only distracted attention from her parents who are caught in a whirlwind of social and business engagements. In her frustrations, she decides to leave home. She gets as far as the train station before the ticket master phones her father. He comes down to retrieve her. The following scene is presented:

> He saw his daughter through the station window. The girl, sitting on the bench, the rich names on her paper suitcase, touched him as it was in her power to touch him only when she seemed helpless or when she was very sick. Someone had walked over his grave! He shivered with longing, he felt his skin coarsen as when, driving home late and alone, a shower of leaves on the wind crossed the beam of his headlights, liberating him for a second at the most, from the literal symbols of his life—the buttonless shirts, the vouchers and bank statements, the order blanks, and the empty glasses. . . . Then, as it was with the leaves, the power of her figure to trouble him was ended; his goose-flesh vanished. He was himself.[2]

Moments of intense intimacy are often that fleeting. The excitement of the other can come from a place, a book, an antique chair. Usually such moments come with another person. Ideally in the present schema of things they come—most frequently come—with one's spouse.

The reality is, of course, that a married couple does not go around "I-Thouing" each other several times a day. Twice a day would be fine, thank you. How about once a week? Would you believe once a month?

A couple must nurture a positive life with each other at the "I-you" level. Spouses must treat each other with care and respect. They must place a high priority on the other's feelings, goals, intentions, and happiness. If they are successful at that level, the more intimate life will follow.

The dance of intimacy truly is maddening. On the one hand a couple must reach for the intimacy. They should help it along. It usually does not come if it is intently pursued. Its existence is too fragile to tolerate such direct action. The couple determined to celebrate their eighth wedding anniversary, the parent embarrassing the teenage son by admitting to self-doubts, the empty nest parents trying to share their interests in life—all can attest to the futility of the pursuit. However, there is a need to try. The very effort assures the other and the self that the intimacy is important.

If the life together is there, however, the moments will come. Who knows how frequently? The circumstances of each couple and of each family are so diverse. The engines which drive the couple, the fuel which feeds the mutual life are also quite diverse:

Scenario One: The Young Marrieds

The younger married couple has passion and newness and excitement urging them toward each other. They are each energized by the newness of their own individual adult person. Their personal energy compels them to look for contact and encounter. Their bodily energy, their lust, strongly urges them to seek contact with others.

They are driven in a very positive way to reach out. The young married couple lacks, however, the comfortableness, the history, the skills, the bonding of years that makes the intimacy very easy. The very energy often drives them past each other—sometimes into the arms of another. Often they do not have a time in which they can develop the skills for being husband and wife. Often children come on the scene before they break in their wedding rings. They often become mommy and daddy before they learn how to be husband and wife.

The very force of their life during this time might well lead to more moments of intimacy than at other periods in their married life. By contrast, the more volatile base of their life can also cause more violent and more frequent periods of distance.

Scenario Two: The Mid-Life Marriage

The bodily and psychological drives which were such allies in the young marrieds' dance with each other now turn to at best questionable assets. There is much going on in the life of the typical mid-life spouse. Often the dynamics can cause so much turmoil within that they have quite a difficult time reaching out toward each other. As they give up their primary roles of mommy and daddy, they must turn toward each other as husband and wife once again or perhaps for the first time or face a destruction of their marriage.

The typical woman in her late forties faces a continually changing body whose hormonal shifts and creeping wrinkles and sags cause her to struggle in a culture that worships hard bodies. A woman at this age, even if she had a career, faces the empty nest. More than likely her main identity has been as mother. Her work outside the home was often secondary to the husband's and was more job than career. With the children gone, even if there was a little glee felt as they walked out the door, the woman must develop a new focus for her life. As she turns toward a career, there is often a cultural and economic barrier between the spouses. She is putting aside the job and looking for a career. He is well up the ladder. All these changes cause self-doubt in her; and at the moment when she needs assurances, often her husband is experiencing a decline in his sexual drive which she can easily translate into a loss of interest in her. To top it all off, just as the children are leaving the nest, often the woman must face the challenge of aging parents. That challenge requires a great deal of dedication as well as quite an identity adjustment.

The man working through his fifth decade has his own crazies to face. His hormonal shifts may not be as dramatic, but the male often has greater difficulty adjusting to the role of a more vulnerable life. The stronger the macho image, the greater the adjustment. He may be well up the ladder of his career, but he also must realize that there will be limits to his achievements. Perhaps his shift from father to spouse may not be as traumatic as the wife's since the kids were only one of the claims on his time. But he may also realize that he missed his kids' childhood. They have left the nest, and he has spent more time in his career than with his children. It is an opportunity that cannot be retrieved. There can be much regret.

With the kids gone, mommy and daddy must turn toward each other and say hi. That is a difficult thing to do given all the other struggles they are going through. Fortunately, they have some things going for them which the young marrieds do not. They have a history together. They have a bonding in which their identities are intertwined. They hopefully have learned much about each other. They hopefully have developed skills in relating. In other words, if they have not been just mommy and daddy, their desire and their need for each other can carry them through the challenges they face.

Scenario Three: The Twilight Years

The couple are in their late seventies/early eighties. He has a pacemaker. He had a hip replaced in his sixties. She had to help him out of a depression at that time. His gall bladder and appendix are out. There are early signs of Alzheimer's disease.

She is doing rather well, thank you. She needs a little help hearing. Her eyes have faded and work only with the aid of some strong lenses. Fifteen years earlier she had a bout with breast cancer. He stood by her, and they made it through.

Each month finds one or two of their friends or acquaintances passing on. They are afraid as they feel more and more fragile. They feel vulnerable. They are afraid for themselves. They are afraid for each other. They are also bored and annoyed with each other as their world shrinks more and more to the four walls of their apartment. It becomes difficult to remain involved in the many settings that have benefited from their active lives. All the worry, all the time together has led to a lot of argument. They probably snip at each other more now than at any other time of their life. There are even moments when they simply do not like each other.

Their life together, however, is a good example of how intimacy is a deeper reality than just the immediate conscious exchange. Their lives are irreversibly intertwined. The identity of one is locked into the life of the other. They are at least as intimate as the young romantic couple drunk with the look, the presence, the smell, and the feel of each other. Arguably, the older couple is more intimate even though they could use some different company to give variety to their day. They are one with each other at the deepest of levels.

Intimacy, therefore, takes on different dynamics as people pass through different stages of their relationship. There is in fact no one reality called intimacy. The word is used to capture the dance people do with each other in an attempt to draw close.

Before people can draw close to each other, of course, they have to achieve other qualities in their life. They have to like themselves at least to a minimal degree. They have to be able to trust other people. In short, before they can reach out to others in the demands of marriage, they have to have experienced enough love and enough success in their dealings with others and with themselves. A person has to be loved before he or she can love. Marriage is a poor place to learn the basic skills of love and intimacy. It is the place where the advanced lessons take place.

What is most paradoxical about the search for intimacy is that it is a disaster if the spouses give up their own individuality. One marries the other, ideally in our society, because the other is different and interesting. Some people then turn to marriage and spend their efforts trying to become the same. A relationship does not have many healthy prospects, however, if the two do not differentiate themselves at the very same time they are trying to engage in the dance of intimacy.

Edwin Friedman makes this point rather strongly in his book *Generation to Generation:*

> Distancing comes about because there is not enough distance to begin with. Marriage partners may separate because they have grown distant, but most couples probably separate because they are not able to achieve any separation at all. Children may wind up undisciplined because their parents pay them no heed, but as many are problemed because they are the objects of too much investment. Emotional distance is perplexing. If there is too much, it is not possible to have a relationship; if there is not enough separation, it is also not possible to have a relationship.[3]

The Christian Perspective

The greatest message that the Christian tradition can bring to the marriage relationship today is a message of failure. It should plead with people to realize that even the most admirable person has significant faults. Every person in the scriptures failed or had doubts in his or her love and service of God. The Christian message should warn people that marriage will not be easy.

The Christian message is not a depressing one. It is not meant to preach doom and despair. Rather, the message of failure is deemed necessary to assure the possibility of success. It becomes a key part of the Christian message today because of contemporary culture's impatience with anything but immediate success. In another place or another time the emphasis might be placed on other aspects of the Christian tradition. Today, however, there is such an intense pursuit of immediate happiness. There is a demand for immediate success. And there is such an impatience with the limitations of life, especially the limitations of others. It is no wonder why marriages are so frail.

The pursuit of self leads to an unhappy narcissism. The pursuit of the other leads to intense joy and intense frustration and anger. The joy cannot be discounted. The frustration and anger must be faced and made productive rather than destructive.

The Christian message does not leave one with the message of defeat, of course. Any caution against unbridled romanticism must be immediately balanced with the sense that people are worth any effort. Not only are people made in the image and likeness of God, but so also is one's lover. The Christian message should cause an excitement about the depth and beauty of the other person. Paradoxically, while the Christian message warns about the limitations of married life, it is at the same time most positive. Nothing is more sensational than the realization that the other is anchored in the deepest mystery of life. Even if the other is fat, gray, and a little slow on the upbeat, the other is seen as residing in God.

Christianity should be one of the forces, then, that combats a certain nervous consumerism. The world is not there to be experienced and used. The world is a community that resides within the ground of all being. It is a community in God. All others—humans, long-haired wambas, white birches, and a fog blanketing a marsh—express the God that is at the base of all creation. They all offer the call of life.

Some, of course, have a greater potential for expressing the depth of life. Humans according to the Christian message have a special place in creation. In fact people become absorbed in each other because it is such a powerful avenue in the search for an intensity in life.

Marriage then is seen as a place where people can find each other if they have the patience, the understanding, and the tolerance to work with each other. Perhaps given the dynamics of the people involved or given the circumstances that deal the cards of life, a couple cannot make it together. If a couple is going to make a success of life, however, they are going to have to be patient, gentle, and forgiving with each other. The God of scripture would have had to walk away from humans many times if patience and understanding were absent.

B. The Search Through Sexuality

Sex is an unruly power that must be contained. Sex is a vital sign of a healthy and enjoyable life that must be maintained. These two contrasts mark the struggle of western culture's attitude toward sexuality.

If one reads material up to the beginning of this century, sex, whether the author be Augustine or Freud, is seen as a truly momentous power. As such it is presented as a threat to the necessary order. Augustine and many of the early writers of the church saw sex as a drive that could propel people into immoral behavior. Sexual appetites had to be resisted at every turn lest they bring down eternal damnation on those pursuing the pleasures of the body which automatically caused harm to the soul.

Freud, of course, was not interested in the immortal soul. He saw the sexual appetites as fundamental drives of life that must be given expression. However, he did realize that people must live in a society. As such, they must learn not to repress their drives but to sublimate them. Every lust and every hatred, every love and every fear cannot be acted upon. To live in society requires redirection in the name of harmony.

There were groups, obviously, who pursued the pleasures of life with abandon. Throughout most of the common era, however, they did not receive center stage. The spotlight generally belonged to people who counseled reasonableness and control as the humans faced a source of inexhaustible energy—sexuality.

Even where control was not a primary counsel, the persistence of the sexual drive was presumed. The pleasure seekers generally agreed with their counterparts that the sexual appetites would always be there to urge the human on to seek greater and greater expression. For those who pursued pleasure with abandon, the sexual appetites were seen as a truly marvelous rollercoaster with an unending source of power. There is not too much of ancient literature that dwells on the loss of sexual powers.

Today, however, sexuality is a power that people worry about for a different reason. True, mothers still worry about their sons being led to disgrace by the accursed itch that knows no satisfaction. True, fathers worry that their little seventeen year old daughters will become big bellied before their socially accepted time. There are even support groups now to help people who are addicted to sex in much the same way as those support groups which help people who are addicted to chemicals or to gambling.

There is recognition, therefore, of the fact that sexual drives can be unruly. However, there is also a change in the setting. Sexual desires are not presumed in present experience; and when they are gone, there is not a lot of dancing and celebration in either the bedroom or the doctor's office. Sexual desires and in some sense sexual activity are seen as signs of a healthy physical and personal life. Part of every extended medical exam probes the vitality of the sexual life. It is seen as a measuring rod. If one's appetites are not alive and active, then the patient either has some physical problems, some interpersonal problems, or simply suffers the stress of a burdensome life. In any case, the powers of the sexual appetites are not assumed or taken for granted. There is a whole body of literature which discusses its demise with great concern.

Eugene Kennedy notes the anxiety in his book, *Sexual Counseling:*

> One must distinguish between an absolute lack of sexual drive and an inhibited condition which may be explained psychologically. An absolute lack of sex drive is, according to Dr. Martin Goldberg of the University of Pennsylvania Medical School, an example of *primary impotence.* This is a condition in which an individual has never experienced sexual drive nor any successful physical sexual reactivity. This is distinguished from *secondary impotence* which occurs in a person who has previously been sexually potent. . . .[4]

The contrast is significant. Upon the demise of a monk's sexual drive, the community of St. Columbanus Monastery in eleventh century Wales would celebrate the true generosity of God's grace. The curse of concupiscence, or at least its most dramatic expression, had been lifted. The monk could be assured of living the remaining years without one of life's more troublesome demons. Today, by contrast, any person who has lost all sexual desire for a considerable length of time would be considered a prime candidate for either physical or psychological treatment.

Certainly, as the archaeologists in the year 5000 AD try to piece together our society, they probably will not find us any more balanced in our view of sexuality than the eleventh century Christians. The medieval setting presented sexuality as a demon to be spurned. Today the culture treats sexuality as an almost divine power to be experienced. Deep down common sense keeps saying that both positions are ridiculous, but sexuality is so basic to our identity as humans that it defies any reasonable approach.

Humans are physical creatures. Everything about the body continually affects who they are and how they are seen. If a person is tall or short, considered attractive or not by others, or is living through the ravages of a body that is changing dramatically with puberty or old age, that person is changed to the very core of life. It is not a question that one's body is changed and therefore one's personality has changed. That is too dualistic. One's person does not sit back and dialogue with one's body. A person's body is an intricate part of a person.

This wholeness must be realized before any discussion can grasp the central importance of sexuality in marriage. In a sense, people marry not simply for intimacy but for sex. They do not marry for the more dramatic form of sex—genital sexuality. Contrary to the norms of most mainstream Christian positions, many experience genital sexuality outside of marriage. But if one takes the broader view of sexuality to include the makeup that is normally termed masculine and feminine, then people marry to put themselves in touch with the rhythms of the other which complement and amplify their own. There is more to this symphony of relationships than the dance of the masculine and feminine. The gender roles, however, are a key part of any relationship.

Genital sexuality in marriage plays so many roles that it is difficult to address them in a single segment of a chapter. Physical intimacy is usually a way of reaching for each other in a dramatic attempt to be close. The list, however, of the different functions that sexuality plays in the history of a marriage is a varied one:

1. A means of climaxing a sense of togetherness and intimacy.
2. A way of making up after an estrangement or an argument.
3. An act that relieves the sexual tensions or desires.
4. An action in which the spouses wrestle with the anger and frustration of the other.
5. A way of paying the other back for kindnesses and favors in their common life.
6. A performance of duty realizing the needs of the other.
7. A tactic to keep the other faithful.
8. A way of having a child.

This list is by no means complete. The reality is, of course, that any single act of physical intimacy probably would include a number of these intentions. Reality loves to defy the orderly classifications of reason.

The challenges posed by sexuality in general and genital sexuality in particular for a marriage in our society are significant. Obviously the present concern with the loss of sexual powers underscores just how important they are. Paradoxically, the obsessive importance placed on genital sexuality can also cause its demise. For years wives used to complain that they had to compete against the foldouts of *Playboy*. Today, however, men have their own competition. Couples are swamped by the scenes of passionate love splashed on the screen, celebrated in song, and detailed in stories. It is difficult for John and Mary not to look around and wonder why they are not keeping pace with the torrid scenes of the media.

If any single element is lost in the present frenzy of sexuality, it would probably be a sense of ritual. A ritual is an action that should be moving and impressive in its actions, but which has an ulterior goal it wishes to celebrate or achieve. There is a passage in *The Little Prince* which is as effective a presentation of ritual as any other.[5]

The story is told of a fox that meets the Little Prince. The fox is lonely and wants to be tamed, but the Little Prince has no idea how to tame anybody. That is probably why he is so lonely. He has not learned how to make someone special, to make someone "unique in all the world." The fox therefore proceeds to develop a ritual whereby they could become tamed or unique for each other.

Each day they are to meet. At first the distance between them will be significant. They will look at each other. On succeeding days they will move ever so closer as they come to gaze upon and develop a sense of the other as a special person. But there is more to the ritual than that simple ceremony as the Little Prince finds out upon his return the second day. The fox tells him that it would have been better had the little visitor returned at the same hour. Such regularity would offer the thrill of anticipation. They both could savor the excitement of the impending meeting.

The fox and the prince tame each other. They become special for each other through the gentle and gradual ritual or rite that they devised. The gentleness, sensitivity, and subtlety of their meetings are essential parts in achieving the delicate beauty of their relationship. The Little Prince would not have succeeded had he simply chained the fox and brought it into his household. Similarly, Tim and Tammy probably hurt their chances of becoming special for each other or even becoming unique for each other if they lack the patience in personal ritual before they bond together in physical intimacy.

The tale of the Little Prince is a difficult one for Boy and Girl to appreciate as they roll in the sack after their third meeting. Often the impatience of our society makes it almost impossible to appreciate how subtle and fragile human relations truly are. The taming, the intimacy comes only with developing common rhythms in life. Trying to force the personal closeness through intimate physical acts often can cause distrust either in oneself or in the sexual partner. If a person blurts out expressions of deepest love and realizes that truly the deepest bond is not present, there is a loss. If a person expresses deep intimacy and believes it is there after a brief relationship only to find the relationship quickly ending, it is difficult to proclaim love in the next relationship. A jilted lover begins to question the meaning of love.

The tale of the Little Prince and the fox does not apply simply to premarital situations. It challenges all to appreciate the reality that sex is truly a ritual in which two people are reaching for something deeper while at the same time being fully involved in the drama of the ritual.

The Christian Perspective

There has been a true dialogue between Christianity and the modern culture on the place of sexuality in human life. In its earliest roots, the Old Testament, the tradition accepts sexuality as a part of God's plan. The second chapter of Genesis speaks of "the two of them become one body." (Gen 2:24) Along with birth and death, the bodily fluids as well as the basic drives of genital sexuality are associated with the power of God. There developed a whole code of cultic purity laws governing human participation in religious services based on actions and the bodily discharges associated with sex.

Sexuality in the Old Testament was a part of life planned by God. As such, though, sexual expression could not be left to the individual whim. Sexual conduct could not be dictated by mere private choice, for the fabric of the people was woven by the sexual interaction of family members. It had to be regulated not primarily because of some challenging personal moral ethic. Rather, the purity and dependability of the family line demanded that sexual activity among Israelites be carefully regulated.

The laws governing human sexual behavior which get fairly specific in the Old Testament had little to do with the present day concern for moral degradation. The Old Testament places no restrictions on the sexual activity of Israelite men provided they do not involve Israelite women. What was important for the Israelites was how the families and thus the social structure of the people were affected.

Sexual activity, then, was not considered in terms of its part in the formation of a lofty moral character. The earliest Israelites were often

most concerned with the basic needs of life. As the Old Testament literature developed, however, there emerged a more idealistic sense of the
human calling. The increased sense of human dignity was marked by an
awareness of the need for personal integrity and fidelity in human conduct in general and in marriage in particular. For most of the literature,
however, questions of sexual morality would more appropriately be
concerns with the purity of the line and the rights of the family of origin.
There is little in the early books of the Old Testament that could be used
for a handbook of sexual morality for Christians today.

In the New Testament, again there is little concern for questions
dealing directly with sexual issues. Pertinent passages here and there in
the gospels, in Paul, and in other books of the New Testament can be
culled from the texts. But there is no systematic presentation of a code of
sexual conduct. The New Testament was concerned with far more important issues than sexual conduct. True, the gospels present Jesus as
celibate. His lifestyle is presented as a testimony to the intensity with
which he pursued the work of his Father. It is not presented as a direct
comment on the values of sexual conduct.

Jesus was absorbed completely in the work of his Father. He called
the disciples to a similar life of uncompromising dedication. There are
several passages throughout the gospels in which one is supposed to
reject every call of this world. In Luke 18:29 a wife is specifically mentioned as something that must be put aside by the disciples of Jesus.

Turning to Paul, the language gets more specific. In a very direct
passage to the Corinthians, discussed in the second chapter of this volume, Paul speaks of marriage as a cure for the pangs of lust. He counsels
marriage for those who cannot follow the better call of celibacy. Like
Jesus, he felt that the Father's business was more important than any
earthly task. Since the second coming of Jesus was expected within the
lifetime of the average Christian, who would want to be distracted by
the cares of this world?

In this specific letter, Paul was also trying to give practical advice to
a Christian community struggling in one of the most notorious cities in
the empire, Corinth. In his attempts to guide the community to a stable
lifestyle, he had little room for singing the praises of the appetites. These
early Christians lived in a society in which frantic pursuit of pleasure
and power pushed that city to the brink of chaos.

Moving out of the scriptures, the previous chapter showed how the
preoccupation with the second coming or the parousia was quickly replaced with the Christian community getting ensnared in the dualism

that was so prominent among those in the empire seeking to call people to a better life.

In the New Testament the eschatological beginnings of Christianity —the sense that there was going to be a monumental new order established by God—simply made sexual questions irrelevant. When the eschatological expectations faded, Christianity was swallowed up in the dualism—the sense of conflict between body and spirit—that has dominated western culture through most of its history. This sense of conflict between the body and the soul made it impossible for the tradition to develop a very positive sense of sexuality. Both the culture as a whole and Christianity in particular had to realize that the body and spirit are intricately one.

The probings of medicine, biology, psychology, and even physics and chemistry have shown that body and spirit cannot be separated. This has led the Christian tradition to appreciate the body as an intricate part of the human.

At the same time that the body/spirit unity has been realized, there has been a growth in appreciating the beauties of the world. Christian reflection has developed primarily in western culture. In the technologically advanced countries of the west, the physical existence of the common person has improved. No longer must the earth be scratched eighteen hours a day for the basics of life. No longer does death wait around the corner for every normal adult. People have room to step back and look at the world and call it good. This positive experience of the world has allowed Christians to appreciate God in the depths of creation.

The previous chapter tried to show the growing appreciation that the tradition has developed for the family as a place which either prepares one to discover God or which provides a direct opportunity to discover God in others—at least in an imperfect way. Parallel to this growing admiration for the family, there has developed an appreciation for the physical intimacy between spouses and between parents and children. More specifically, there has developed a sensitivity for the value played by the sexual intimacy in a couple's life together. Sexual intimacy is seen as a bonding and a healing, a celebrating and a life-giving ritual. Much of this appreciation the church has learned from the culture.

The church has learned much then. It also feels that it must teach much. The church feels called to witness to the bonding, commitment, and fidelity necessary in sexuality. If sexual expression, especially genital sexual expression, is to be life-giving, it must be in a relationship that

promises commitment, intimacy, and fidelity. The degree of sexual intimacy should correspond to the degree of personal intimacy and fidelity.
Otherwise, the physical reaching for each other will more than likely
cause distrust and insecurity rather than growth and love.

C. The Search Through Children

There is a crisis of sorts in most technological western countries.
Many segments of the native population are not replacing themselves.
Certainly, the glaring question globally is not underpopulation. There is
in fact a rampant population explosion that threatens the most basic
quality of life on the earth. Most highly technologically advanced western countries, however, experience growth only through immigration.

Given the worldwide crisis of overpopulation, some might argue
that any decrease in the number of people should be a positive trend.
The question about population trends in the technological west, however, is not one of raw numbers. The concern rests more with the underlying attitudes toward life that give rise to the population patterns. Has
the population refused to say yes to life? Is the decline in new births a
sign of a fear of life? Is it a symptom of a society turned in upon itself in a
pursuit of self-satisfaction and material comforts?

Why is there a reluctance to have children in the technological west?
Not surprisingly, the answer is complex. So too are the facts. The number of women having at least one child today is relatively high. Of the
women born in the United States in 1850 there were 8.5 percent who did
not have children. Of those born at the turn of the century, the percent-
age of women who remained childless was 20. For those born in 1935
the childless rate was 7.3.[6]

Women born in	Childless rate
1850	8.5
1900	20.0
1935	7.3

That pattern is a surprising one for people not familiar with the
history of family in this country. To some extent the increase in the
childless rate for those born at the turn of the century could be explained
by the economic depression which gripped the country when these women would be at child-bearing age. During economically hard times,

there is an expected drop in the number of children. However, such a facile explanation does not fit the pattern. In fact the childless rate witnessed a steady rise throughout the nineteenth century. If the numbers were to be filled in between 1850 and 1900, there would be a steady increase in the childless rate throughout the 1800s. Similarly, if the years were filled in between 1900 and 1935 there would be a steady drop in the childless rate.

To predict the childless rate for women born in the second half of this century is difficult. They have not finished their child-bearing years. Any projection would require flimsy conjecture rather than any intelligent use of facts. There is some indication that the number of childless women has increased. They have not soared.

Again, the question of key concern is: What do these facts mean? What shifts in the human reality do they represent? Were women in the 1800s avoiding children by abstaining from sexual intimacy? Were they avoiding having children through some primitive means of birth control? Were there large numbers of women sterile because of their participation in the industrial revolution? Conceivably, long hours in the factory combined with poor diets and unhealthy living conditions could have taken their toll on the reproductive powers of women.

If there was a conscious practice of birth control prior to the more sophisticated methods which became commonplace in the early 1970s, then the control of births in some sense depended on the cooperation of the male. He either had to consent to continence, or he had to be willing to withdraw prior to climax. There were other means available, but these were the two primary ones. The big change today is that the control of birth can rest mostly with the woman who can, prior to any act of intercourse, take steps to prevent conception. This point is made by Martine Segalen in a study of the question.[7]

Segalen also cites a number of authors to make the very important point that the practice of birth control is so relatively easy and acceptable today that the question has changed. Up until the past two decades there had to be a conscious decision to avoid children. Today's practices have shifted the focus. Today, for most people who give direction to their lives, there has to be a conscious decision to have children. A married couple must alter the practices of their married life if they desire to have offspring.

The results have been dramatic. In the United States the average woman in 1850 would have just under six children. Today the average woman has under two children. Of course, the large majority of those twentieth century children, unlike their nineteenth century counterparts, will live into their adult life. Still, the contrast is telling. And it is not limited to the United States. One study included Canada, Netherlands, France, Great Britain, Sweden, and the Federal Republic of Germany. In each case the average woman in these countries prior to the 1960s would have had over two children in a lifetime. In most cases the fertility rate increased during the 1950s. However, in the early 1960s the birth rate took a noticeable decline to a point where all these countries are significantly below two births per woman. The most dramatic drop took place in Canada where the birth rate dropped from almost four births per woman in the late 1950s to about 1.8 at the close of the 1970s. At the close of that decade the Federal Republic of Germany was just below 1.4.[8]

Country	Average # in 1950	# in 1979
Canada	3.4	1.7
Netherlands	3.1	1.6
France	2.9	1.8
England	2.2	1.8
Sweden	2.3	1.6
Federal Rep.	2.1	1.4

What do such significant shifts say about the desire to have children in the west? What do they say about the present willingness in western technological countries to pass on life? The optimists would say that in western countries there is a greater respect for children. They would point to the education system, the toy industry, the books on child care, the growing respect for the rights of children, the challenge to corporal punishment, and even the more accurate statistics on child abuse. They would look at these institutions and statistics and argue that while we have fewer children, those we have are loved and valued. They are treated, the argument would continue, with more respect than in any other society in history. They are wanted and do not simply happen.

The pessimists would take many of the same realities and insist that in fact the patterns indicate that the society is becoming unglued. For these people, the increase in child abuse cases is not simply a sign of increased sensitivity toward corporal punishment and better vigilance. Rather, it indicates that there is a growing impatience and intolerance on the part of parents who either are unsure of themselves or so turned in upon themselves that they cannot afford the time and consideration for their children. Similarly, these skeptics would turn toward the toy, clothing, and educational industries and argue that they are not true signs of love and concern. Rather, they are the modern equivalents of the boarding schools of past centuries in which the parents of the time would show a willingness to spend their wealth on their children so that they would not have to expend their time and affection.

The Christian Perspective

As with so many specific topics in life, the Christian tradition, incorporated into many different cultures, has displayed a number of attitudes toward children. The tradition does not present a handbook of answers to all the questions of life. Rather, it presents a community in search of God in many different settings. The meaning that a given reality of life—in this case children—has for a people, then, depends at least in some measure on the overall setting.

In the Old Testament, as was shown in the second chapter, children were a source of immortality, prosperity, security, and personal identity. They were considered the main blessing from God and prized over all the other blessings of life. In the New Testament, children were all but ignored in the gospels. In one scene depicted in the synoptic gospels, Jesus turns the value of children around by making them the norm for life. His disciples are told in the scene that unless they become like little children they cannot enter the kingdom. Making children the norm for life flew in the face of the wisdom of the day in which children were seen as creatures struggling to achieve the wisdom of the adults.

Aside from an occasional reference, however, there was not any concentration in the New Testament on the life of children because there was such a fever over the new order expected with the return of Jesus. The domestic concerns simply faded to the background.

Following the first century, it became obvious that the second coming or parousia was not to be within any predictable time. As previous chapters showed, Christianity became enmeshed in the dualistic worldview of the day. Children, as a result, were emphasized in marriage for two reasons. First, the church must continue. There must be children along with converts to keep the church growing. Second, without much of a positive sense of the sexual drive, the only reason for marriage was to have children and thus help to fulfill the plan of God for propagating the human race. The only reason to justify having intercourse even within marriage was to have children. Even toward the close of the middle ages where intercourse in marriage was seen as an acceptable cure for the unruly desires of lust, the partners always had to intend or at least to be open to having children.

As the church grew in its appreciation of the beauties of the physical world, it also saw the value of the sexual exchange between the marital partners. However, the tradition did not lose its reverence for children. Any community which is taken with the mystery and the power of life has a natural reverence for children. Any community which is taken with the power of the sacred in creation must sense the new life of a child as one of the most dramatic expressions of this sacred pulse of life. A birth is one of the most explicit acts of God or at least of God's creative power. Therefore, it is difficult for the community to accept any refusal on the part of its members to have children. The sense of participating in the basic creative mystery through child-bearing is so strong that many in the tradition cannot resonate with any blanket intention to avoid children.

The different churches in the traditions do vary in their reactions to couples who deliberately avoid children. Some simply recognize the freedom of conscience of every Christian and the different workings of God in individual lives. If a couple clearly chooses not to have children, that is simply seen as their choice. Their life, however, should be one that seeks to participate in the passing on of life in other ways.

Other communities in the Christian tradition are much more explicit. The Catholic Church, for example, clearly argues for the place of children in any marriage. Pastorally it counsels a couple who have difficulty seeing themselves as having children. Faced with prospective spouses who categorically refuse to consider having any children, a pastor in the Catholic Church should technically deny marriage. Many priests take a more pastoral approach, however, and realize that a young couple's patterns are subject to significant change with the maturing of their marriage. It is not too difficult for twenty-three year olds to say they are never going to have children since they have so much time to change their minds. It is very difficult for thirty-three year olds to say the same. For people in their mid-thirties such a declaration really means for ever and ever. It is a now or never decision.

All this concern for children was originally expressed in the tradition by calling children the primary end of marriage. The love of the couple was seen as a secondary end. This was particularly true in the Catholic tradition. Presently, though, there is a deliberate attempt to avoid any hierarchy. The love that grows between the family members in general and the spouses in particular is seen as sufficient justification for any marriage. This personal bonding of the spouses is seen as being one end of marriage. Children are seen as an equally important end of marriage.

1. Birth Control.　Actually it is only in this overall context of appreciating children that one can understand the Christian attitudes toward birth control and abortion. For one taken with the presence of God, there is a natural reverence for new life. The sense of God in every birth becomes a riveting reality. At times the reality becomes so moving that the community may appear to lose a balanced perspective.

As the previous chapter showed, the church was very reluctant to accept the practice of birth control. It had a natural affinity for the large family as a celebration of the goodness of God. The church had to realize that the quality of life was as important as the quantity. Given couples could not emotionally and financially handle an unbridled number of children. At some point the quality of life would suffer. A married couple had to recognize the freedom to choose the number of offspring they could love and nourish.

Today virtually all Christian groups recognize the right of the couple to decide how many children they will have. In fact, most communities go one step further and speak of the moral obligation of the parents to assure that they can care for the basic material and educational needs of their children along with sufficient and appropriate love and security. If one is going to have children, there should be a reasonable assurance that these children will receive love and proper care.

There is a tension then in many of the Christian communities. It is particularly evident in the Catholic Church. Its official teaching does not accept artificial means of birth control. It does recognize that a couple could use the natural rhythm of the body to limit the number of children. However, it argues that every act of love must be open to new life. In the reasoning of the Catholic Church, an inherent part of that new life in any act of sexual love is children. Official church documents bemoan what John Paul II decries as a contraceptive mentality. There is a sense that amidst all the good of the present setting, the culture has failed to realize that true growth in anyone's life comes from a willingness to share one's life with another. A person who spends a lifetime being kind and considerate may not have truly lived beyond the self in any intense way. Kind and considerate people can easily isolate themselves enough to assure that no aggressive demands are made on them. In such cases the person has not experienced the intensity of life possible within the Christian calling.

In *Faithful to Each Other Forever,* a book put out by the Bishops' Committee for Pastoral Research and Practices that is designed to be a handbook for those responsible for marriage preparation in the Catholic

Church, one reads the following explanation for insisting on natural family planning:

> The Church has offered and continues to offer clear, challenging, and prophetic—even if controversial—guidance to the husband and wife who are struggling with that sensitive and often difficult issue. It teaches that the act of sexual intercourse has two meanings, which cannot be separated: the unitive meaning, by which the love of a couple is symbolized, sustained, and strengthened; and the procreative meaning, by which the couple open themselves to the possibility of cooperating with God in the creation of a new person. Since these two meanings of the act cannot be separated without undercutting God's design of human sexuality and undermining the total, reciprocal self-giving between spouses, the Church states that "each and every marriage act must remain open to the transmission of new life." As a consequence, it approves natural family planning and rejects as immoral various forms of contraception.[9]

The handbook goes on to explain the different methods of natural family planning and notes through the use of charts their relative effectiveness and safety compared to artificial methods of contraception.

The formal language of theological arguments as well as charts, however, leaves many unmoved. Perhaps the most convincing arguments for natural means of birth control can be found in the personal testimonies of those who use it.

One woman writes the following:

> Once again, what sustains our commitment to NFP [natural family planning] and our desire to breast feed ecologically our children is that the two of us can talk about this as being a hardship. We know that that inconvenience is temporary and that the rewards are tremendous.
>
> As for myself, I have learned so much about my own fertility with its physical, psychological, and emotional effect upon who I am that it has led to greater personal growth. I am not in any way harming my life-giving ability, which God has granted me.[10]

In another example mentioned in the handbook, a husband makes the following comments:

> Continence does me a favor. It provides me with a "rhythmic" opportunity to make sure it is love and intimacy, not sex, which bind me to my wife. This is why I see NFP as being non-chauvinistic, for husband and wife both mutually have to make it work. The periodic tension that sometimes comes with continence means we frequently examine our

relationship, our needs, our communication, and the quality of our intimacy and affection. I am very thankful to have a spouse who loves me and herself enough to demand that I love her in a way that Christian marriage requires.

Thus, fertility acceptance (NFP) not only reminds me of our interpersonal, procreative potential but is a constant reminder that genital intimacy falls in the context of relational intimacy. As a male, that is extremely important, given my natural tendency to overemphasize the quality of the genital relationship.[11]

The handbook goes on to note that natural family planning is not practiced by many. It notes a national survey in which only four percent "responded that they follow natural family planning or periodic abstinence."[12] It continues to note that even among church members there is not widespread acceptance of the teaching. In the words of the handbook, "there is considerable evidence that significant numbers of Roman Catholics in the United States also reject official teaching on this matter."[13]

For many, there is a difficulty in seeing why there should be such a stress on the contrast between artificial and natural means of control.

2. Abortion. The reverence for children is equally indispensable in understanding the community's stance on abortion. Virtually every Christian community starts with the position that abortion is a grave issue. Most counsel against it. Many scream against it. The Christian churches, however, show at least some of the division that characterizes the whole society.

One of the strongest voices against abortion has always come from the Catholic Church. Pope John Paul II speaks of "the scourge of abortion" and insists that "any violence . . . in favor of contraception or, still worse, of sterilization and procured abortion must be altogether condemned. . . ."

In a statement that lumps abortion with other issues about new life, John Paul continues:

> Thus, an anti-life mentality is born, as can be seen in many current issues. One thinks, for example, of a certain panic deriving from the studies of ecologists and futurologists on population growth, which sometimes exaggerate the danger of demographic increase to the quality of life. But the Church firmly believes that human life, even if weak and suffering, is always a splendid gift of God's goodness. Against the pessimism and selfishness which cast a shadow over the world, the

Church stands for life. In each human life it sees the splendor of the "yes," that "amen" who is Christ himself.[14]

The statement pools together a number of issues in which the Catholic Church continues to make its voice heard. There is no doubt that in that list of anti-life practices, abortion clearly receives the strongest condemnation. Abortion is generally presented as the moral equivalent of murder.

Other statements in the Christian tradition are not as categorical in their condemnation of abortion. One of the more open ones within the Christian tradition can be found in the American Lutheran publication, *Sex, Marriage and the Family:*

> In the consideration of induced abortion the key issue is the status of the unborn fetus. Since the fetus is the organic beginning of human life, the termination of its development is always a serious matter. Nevertheless, a qualitative distinction must be made between its claims and the rights of a responsible person made in God's image who is in living relationships with God and other human beings. This understanding of responsible personhood is congruent with the historical Lutheran teaching and practice whereby only living persons are baptized.[15]

This statement stresses the gravity of any decision to abort. It also wants to distinguish clearly between the unborn fetus and an independent living child. This distinction, of course, opens the door to the possibility of abortion because terminating the fetus from this perspective is not the same as killing another person. It is not murder.

The statement captures the agony that Christian groups face as they try to understand the decision of many of their members to have abortions despite the tradition's reverence for new life. The statement is not one that all in the American Lutheran Church accepted at the time of its publication. There are many in the newly merged Evangelical Lutheran Church of America who do not agree with the statement. It does show, however, how a responsible body of Christians does see the possibility of abortion for those who consider themselves followers of Christ.

The agony of the debate can also be found in the American Baptist Church. A position adopted by the church's general board in 1981 begins by noting how the issue throws several of their "historic commitments" in tension. They specifically mention their commitments "to the sanctity of human life," "to freedom of conscience and self-determination," and finally "to the First Amendment guarantee of the free exercise of religion."

They conclude the first part of their statement with the following passage:

> We recognize the moral pain experienced by those individuals considering an abortion and by persons in society whose consciences are distressed by abortion. We recognize the practical and constitutional limits on state power to enforce moral judgments. We also recognize our responsibility to speak out in defense of the sanctity of human life and the sanctity of conscience as moral issues and as questions of public policy.[16]

The churches agree with each other that abortion should be avoided. There is some disagreement, obviously, whether abortion is ever permissible. There is more consensus in the Christian churches than in society taken as a whole. There is not, however, an absence of tension.

D. The Search Through Work and Creativity

It was about seven in the evening after a joyful, long, noisy and rewarding Christmas day. The woman in her early sixties sat with heavy eyes but alert mind in her living room. Most had gone home by now. On the couch, a few feet away, were two of her daughters. They were turned ever so much toward each other and sent a rather quiet rhythmic sound her way as their conversation took subtle dips and turns. It was a pleasing sound to the older woman. She smiled ever so slightly as it reminded her of the soothing sensation she feels when Oreo, her cat, comes purring around her in the morning if she is inconsiderate enough to rest a few minutes past his normal breakfast time.

It had been a long day. She had gotten up at 5:00 AM to be sure the turkey had plenty of time. Preparations, of course, had been going on for several days with shopping, baking, decorating, and the planning of so many details. The schedule during holidays was tight ever since she took that job in the bank about fifteen years ago. In some ways, though, she and Greg, her husband, were closer than ever during the holidays. Where once everything was left to her, the husband and wife now shared the preparations. While the baking was still left to her efforts, he really gave his all to the shopping, decorating, and planning.

She was tired—no question about it. It was a good tired, however. She felt fulfilled, and so did Greg. They felt needed. They felt appreciated. It was not simply a question of being loved. They knew their six children, the five spouses, and the eight grandchildren loved them. These days, though, they had so little opportunity to do things for

others. Everyone had moved out. When they come home they are looking to do things for their parents. It was simply good to see how she
and her husband could create such a sense of happiness in the entire
family.

——————— ◇ ———————

The above vignette is a helpful starting point in capturing the importance of a four letter word. "Work" has never been deleted from
books in decades past because people found it obscene. It is not even a
word which is included in scripts today to give the rhetoric a naughty,
realistic tone. People, however, often do take offense at the thought of
work.

People in their fifties plan deliciously for their retirement and try to
decide if they want to take their "thirty and out." Spouses walk around
with a small cloud over their head as they put off cleaning the bathroom,
cleaning out the drawers, fixing the light switch, or maybe even doing
the dishes. Many yuppies live for Friday nights when they can let loose
at the TGIF party. And, finally, most have seen a discourse of two be-
moaning working mothers who should be spending more time in the
direct care of their children if not their husbands.

There is, of course, another dimension to the reaction to work.
There are people who are workaholics. In a more modest vein, there are
people who genuinely enjoy their jobs. There are retirees who miss their
work and who would gladly go back to the challenge and social life of
their former job. There are other retirees who even before their first
social security check arrives are busy in some other vocation. There are
even people who enjoy cleaning the house or cutting the grass. There is a
certain therapy in their efforts. Work often comes between spouses as
one gets involved in the lure of a job or an avocation while ignoring
the other.

Actually, most would readily admit they need something to do.
People feel the need to keep busy. Most appreciate a certain structure to
their time. The wrinkle appears when the time is too structured and the
deadlines too persistent. While all at one time or another have shared the
tired sense of satisfaction that the two-career older couple did in the
opening vignette, such a Christmas would indeed be unpleasant if it had
to be faced every day.

Those who enjoy their jobs are genuinely envied. All have a strong
fear, buried ever so deep, of being bored. Being overworked is not fun.
Being bored is worse. The trick, then, is to find work that presents variety, reasonable structure, and bearable pressure. Finding such a mix is

no easy task, obviously. Only about a third of the work force enjoy their present jobs.

The changing work scene offers its special challenges to marriage and family life today. In a sense working mothers are not new. Certainly the mother in the agrarian setting did extensive work. Scenes of pastoral bliss present the family sweating together as they earned their daily bread and cemented a common bond. The full truth was probably somewhat harsher with all the members being overtaxed by the demands of daily labor. Often the mother and father would not find the time to properly nurture their children or their own relationship as they collapsed from a brutal day of trying to survive. Negatively, the harsh demands of survival often made the gentler, nourishing side of marriage and family life more difficult to achieve. Negatively, the family working in the same surroundings and the same structured world could easily become turned in upon themselves. Positively, there was the bond that came from depending on each other to meet the challenge of life's demands.

With the onset of the industrial revolution the task of the work became quite different. Now the family was separated as the members went to labor in different settings for wages that had to be used for the purchase of goods from others. Perhaps the work in the newly developed factories was no less brutal. How can such things truly be measured? Surely accounts of the early industrial centers into the closing decades of the nineteenth century leave little doubt about how crushing the conditions in most factories and mines were for the humanity and of course the families of the men, women, and children who had to work under these conditions. Work was hard on marriages. Work was hard on family life.

With the onset of a more flourishing economy and greater quantities of material goods, there developed greater controls over the conditions of working life. First, governments controlled the more evident abuses through child labor laws and other guidelines that were meant to offer the basic protection for the laborer. Later, unions were successfully organized, and further control was brought upon the working place. Attempts were made to assure a greater distribution of the profits. In this context there was a significant drop in the number of children and women in the work force.

What the shifts in the early decades of this century did in effect was to re-establish the man in his traditional role as head of the family. With the wife and children now located more explicitly in the domestic setting and dependent upon the father for their material needs, the man's position as head was once again clearly established. It was a position that was assumed in the agrarian culture since the male was the stronger of the two spouses in a lifestyle that naturally depended upon physical strength for its success.

In some ways the decades of the first half of the twentieth century were among this country's most domestic despite the interruption of two world wars. The family was touted as the cornerstone of the nation, and there was every effort made to maintain it as a stable institution—at times even where this meant that dysfunctional families were held together.

With the onset of the recent decades, however, the setting has changed. The internationalization of the economy has required that western workers now compete with the salaries and working conditions of developing countries. Many of these countries face conditions that characterized the industrial beginnings of western countries. In fact, the conditions are often worse. The controlling wealth is often found outside the country and is much more difficult to regulate.

There are two dramatic changes in marriage and family life, then, that have occurred in this new internationalized economic setting. First, the work of the laborer has lost significant financial ground. In order to maintain the lifestyle that has become the expected norm, it is now necessary, at least in the minds of most spouses, for both to work at least part time. This means that the spouses are separated from each other and from their children for a large portion of the day. The work place, therefore, has a significant impact on the relationship of the spouses. The demands of the job also raises the question of who is caring for the children.

The second dramatic change has seen a shift in the relative values of the work skills. The economy is now more technological and service oriented and not as industrially based. This has shifted the potential worth of the male and female. No one is so naive as to suggest that there is de facto equality of the sexes in the work force. The feminization of poverty is a clear testimony to how far the system must still change. Old systems die hard. The shift, though, when the 1980s are compared to the 1950s, is dramatic, irreversible, and in its early stages. Women have certain disadvantages in the world of careers since the joy and challenge of child-bearing falls much heavier on them and since the culture still offers less incentive to the woman to pursue a career. The bottom line, however, is that women should continue to grow in the work force in general and in the more responsible and lucrative positions in particular. Physical strength and size are not the economic assets they once were.

Basic intelligence and social graces are the two most important assets in the marketplace. Women are the equal of men in the first and perhaps have a slight edge in the second.

The implications of these shifts in the marketplace are many. The modern marriage, partly as a result of this growing economic equality, has a greater emphasis on mutuality and partnership. Ideally, at least, within the culture as a whole the man is not seen as the head of the household.

The Christian Perspective

From a Christian point of view, the need for work is not hard to understand. There is a deep persistence throughout the gospels that one cannot turn toward pleasing the self. The sense of God in life urges all to seek a broader, richer experience of life. All are called to live beyond themselves in the service of God and their fellow humans. Work is one of the ways of living beyond the self.

The Christian axiom, "Whoever would save his life will lose it, but whoever loses his life for my sake will find it" (Mt 16:25), summarizes the call. Neither the statement nor the reality is very simple. The statement is a paradox, and the reality it reaches is truly maddening.

There is an understandable urge in our individualistic society to collapse the paradox. The sweet reasonableness of our day leads people to realize that they help others because it makes them feel good. Such a simple version of enlightened selfishness does not capture the richness of the gospel challenge, however. A person cannot simply give of the self either in work, in love, or in some form of creativity with the conviction that he or she will be happy. Often in the crunch of giving every available effort, there is no reassuring picture of personal return. The paradox runs even deeper. One cannot even be looking for the personal return because that is not truly living beyond the self. Such a measured effort never discovers the joy that comes with truly giving of the self.

At other times in the Christian tradition, the paradox would be collapsed in the opposite direction. The Christian church simply counseled self-sacrifice. The self was seen as the source of the trouble, and the individual Christian was encouraged to simply renounce the self. However, today's church has learned enough from modern psychology to appreciate the original paradox of the gospels. People cannot live a life in which they simply feel they are being drained. Their lives soon deteriorate into bitterness and anger. Somehow people must have a sense of the growth in their life. They must sense a growth in the Spirit of God, in their own personal spirit, or at least in their relationship with the world and other people.

Therein lies the secret of why many do not find their work fulfilling. Some never get beyond worrying about themselves or their rights or the amount of work they do. Others, however, are in situations where they cannot sense that growth of life no matter how freely they give. They cannot sense themselves growing in the Spirit of God. They cannot sense the growth of their own spirit. They cannot sense a growth in their relationship with others. All three growths—in the Spirit of God, in the individual spirit, and in the relationship with others—are indeed one reality. They do represent different levels at which one can appreciate life. People need to experience growth in their work at one level at least.

When there is an experience of growth somewhere in the process, work can be a true experience of fulfillment. It can provide an opportunity and a stimulus to develop individual talents as one relates with others either in direct service, in the social setting of shared tasks with fellow workers, or simply in the creative efforts or working with the materials of this world.

1. Domestic Work in Marriage and Family Life. Family in our society is meant to be a community of intimacy. It is the place where people seek a closeness and an intensity that are seldom matched in other relationships. Family members, however, do not simply sit around being close. They develop varying degrees of intimacy as they do the curious dance of sharing life. A healthy family, then, among its many skills, must learn how to share its communal tasks. It is important that some working together takes place. It is important that members of the family have a chance to be of service to each other.

One of the challenges to modern life is finding opportunities to be together. So much of the present rhythm of life draws individual family members away from the home. Parents have careers; children are at school; parents go out with friends on the weekend; children belong to the scouts or a sports team. Finding opportunities to be together is of great importance. A common project in the house creates a common interest. People cannot simply sit down and talk. They have to have something to talk about. They have to share common tasks, or there is no common life.

One cannot press too hard for common projects. The skills and interests of different family members vary greatly. It is simply a sense of appreciating the times, many of them quite modest, when there can be a common task. If the opportunity arises when children and parents can share a job, then one should encourage the communal effort even if the job could be done as easily by one. Again, the caution is not to press too hard to make work projects or to force a mutuality of effort. The contrived in human efforts is easily recognized as such and seldom appreciated.

Individual work also plays a part in cementing the domestic scene. Again, family members do not sit around loving each other. They must have an opportunity to share life. They must have moments when they can do for each other. Work done for the benefit of all or for another individual member of the family helps the worker and the benefactor experience the caring and concern in the concrete. Working for another after a falling out can be a most effective way of expressing sorrow. Working for another after a moment of intimacy can express how much one appreciated the moment of sharing.

2. Two Professional Careers in Marriage and Family Life. The Christian vision insists that the individual who is in frantic pursuit of self-fulfillment is doomed to a life of unhappiness. It must be equally insistent that the family cannot be content with seeking its own needs and wants. Any healthy family must find some way of serving others as a family unit or of supporting individual members in their work and service. The family community will soon die on the vine if the fruits of its labors do not benefit others.

Not all reflections on work and the family appreciate this call to service. Work is often presented as a threat to family life. Either the all-consuming career of one working spouse is singled out for attack, or the hectic and disruptive day in the life of the two-career family is held up for analysis. Careers are often seen as necessary evils to provide the material goods for the family's needs.

The reality is, however, that most people, even those who do not like their present job and even those who thoroughly enjoy their family life, want successful careers. There seems to be a basic instinct that affirms a good job as a way of enriching life. The question for the present concerns must be the impact that careers can have on the family.

Certainly, the tension and the stress associated with arousing two adults and three children each day at 6:00 AM does not appear to be a good foundation for a healthy family life. Each morning there has to be a tight schedule as everyone struggles to wash, dress, eat, and attend to the other necessities of life. The husband catches the bus. The youngest is dropped off at the day school by mom on the way to her job. The two elementary school students must wait at home by themselves for twenty minutes until the school bus arrives at the corner. Certainly there are better ways of starting the day.

People must decide what the necessities and opportunities of their life demand. Many families feel they have no choice but to have both spouses working. Others simply choose to have both spouses working because they feel they will be happier. Without analyzing the whys and wherefores of two career families, there are potential benefits to the marriage relationship and the family's overall health.

In our society people marry because they find each other interesting, alive, and fun. Early in the marriage, the realities of life might come crashing down on the couple. They will probably soon learn that any marital relationship involves a much more complex mix of virtues and faults. Unlike traditional societies, however, where one married for primarily economic and social reasons, today people marry for intimacy or at least companionship. Traditional societies might introduce the prospective spouses shortly before their marriage and give them the mandate to learn to love each other. Modern society allows two people to choose their own spouses who in some way are supposed to be soul mates. The one resonates with the other. The two feel that they can be happy together.

The reality is not all that ideal. Perhaps the present culture has a chip on its shoulder as it searches life for its right to be happy. But to some extent these protestations are not relevant to the issue. In reality the culture creates expectations in us that must be taken seriously. Most of us do marry because we like the spirit and bounce of the other. The attractiveness and excitement of the other makes the commitment and experience of love easier.

The reality, of course, is that we change. The person we marry at the age of twenty-four is not the same at the age of fifty. To some extent we owe each other, as far as lies in our power and circumstances, to keep those elements alive in us which attracted the spouse in the first place. To simply adjust our lives to meet the needs and demands of other family members will ensure that many of our unique qualities will wither on the vine of accommodation.

Under the right circumstances two careers can contribute to the marriage because they keep both partners alive and involved in life. The husband and wife have a lot to talk about as they share the rhythms and events of their work. Their careers also help avoid the uneven development found in partners where the working spouse is reaching the height of his or her career in the early fifties of their life and the domestic spouse is feeling rather disoriented after the nest is empty.

Even the tension associated with such a two-career marriage can be a stimulus to growth provided it is not overwhelming. The challenge is to find ways of managing the pieces of their busy lives. The challenge is to support the other when things are not going well. Lives without challenge are lives that can easily settle into the lowest common denominator.

Some may accept that two-career families can prove helpful for selected marriage relationships; however, they may protest, the children are the sure losers. Latchkey kids who must leave and/or arrive at empty houses may learn good lessons in self-reliance or in helping their parents. They can also show problems as they try to fit into the busy schedules of their parents. Certainly, such an argument would proceed, whatever narrow benefits that would accrue to the immediate marital relationship would have to be weighed against the toll it takes on the lives of the children.

The benefit to the children of two-career families should not be too readily dismissed. To some extent the impact on children depends on many factors within the family. First, there are the obvious benefits in educational and material benefits to the children. Second, there is the important question of role models for both the boys and girls in a family. Children who have a mother working in a career comparable to the father's have an easier time sensing the equality of women. Girls who are pondering their own lives have more of a stimulus to realize their true potential. Boys who come from such a home environment will more readily accept the talents of women and will be more likely to respect women throughout their adult life both in the workplace and at home.

More immediate rewards, however, can be seen in the growing years of the children. Parents who are happier with their individual lives will generally be better parents. Children can sense the happiness in others just as adults can. A person who is basically at peace brings a more positive attitude and spirit to the way he or she relates. One who already has achieved a happiness in life can benefit even more from a relationship with immediate family members.

In assessing the impact of two careers on a family, then, the first question must be: How positive are the work experiences? Studies indicate that women who work report a slightly higher satisfaction with their lives than those who do not. No similar studies exist for men, but one would assume a similar result. At any rate there are clear benefits for both spouses in a two-career family. Both would have the freedom to take jobs that pay less but are more personally rewarding. Similarly, both might be able to opt for a job that allows more time with the family. Finally, in face of a job termination for one spouse, the trauma to the family would not be as draining. There would be at least one salary to fall back on.

All these possibilities translate into potentially happier, less pressured parents. In turn, the children benefit from parents who bring to their parenting a more positive attitude and a less pressured atmosphere to the family life.

3. Single Career Marriage and Families. The single-career marriage and family could consist of either the single parent supporting the children or the couple, possibly with children, in which one spouse works. Some of the questions facing these two situations are obviously different. There is considerable overlap.

In both situations, the domestic setting benefits from the income of the member employed outside the home. But besides supplying income and a sense of financial security, the employed member of the family often presents the stimulus to the domestic setting. What is the economy like? What are the political issues at stake? What are the racial and ethnic tensions alive in the community? What interesting products are on the market or being developed? These are some of the issues that the employed member brings to the family dinner table, the living room conversation, and the occasional remarks.

Members of the family may not be individually absorbed in these topics. The issues may not find their way often into the center of attention. They will, to some degree, however, be a part of the life of the employed member. They will be raised from time to time with accompanying comment.

It is important that such topics are raised for children, for one of the most effective ways that children learn is by listening to the conversation of parents. Children may not even participate in the conversation. Still their socialization process draws heavily upon the conversations of their parents and other adults. It is necessary for Christians to have a social conscience. If a child is not brought up where the greater concerns of the world are mentioned, then the social imagination is not nurtured in the early crucial years.

The life of any marriage, the life of any family in general, needs this input from the larger community. Many families readily turn in upon themselves and abdicate any concern, awareness, or responsibility for the life of the larger community. As mentioned earlier, the Christian vision warns that the individual life suffers when it turns in upon itself. So does a marriage and a family which shut off the contact with the larger community.

The employed member thus brings more to the domestic setting than simply material goods. The domestic setting in turn must do its share in supporting the employed member. The family presents the care, love, and unconditional acceptance that cannot be readily found in the commercial world. That is easily recognized. The unemployed (as distinct from non-working) members of the family, however, should provide another dimension. The spouse as well as the children who center their lives primarily around the home can offer more than simply the caring and nurturing so readily associated with the home. The domestic setting can be a constant reminder of how one must pause and find fulfillment in the others who are close.

The mother who remains at home with three small children must face as many challenges in the daily routine of life as the employed father. But she must find her fulfillment in dealing with the small, the mundane, the relational, the non-dramatic. She must learn how to love amidst the spilt oatmeal and the fighting children. She must cope with picking up the room for the thirteenth time by early afternoon not because her job requires order but simply because she desires order.

Similarly, the spouse who for one reason or another remains at home even though there are no children must also find meaning and fulfillment in the simple and the immediate. Often the world is quiet. Often the world involves solitude. Often such a spouse must find the secret that keeps the solitude from turning into boredom and loneliness.

The elements or challenges of the domestic spouse are not those that normally fill the day of the employed worker. The work place is characterized more often by the highly structured, the dramatic, the prescribed repetitive, or the clearly productive. Often the one who spends the greater part of the day in the commercial world does not have the skills or secrets necessary to discover the dimensions available to those who cope in the domestic world.

The two have much to learn from each other. Work permeates our lives. It is the way people fulfill their stewardship. It is the way individuals can carry out some of the dimensions of God's work in the world. Some would find the term co-creators with God as being too arrogant, but at the very least work is the way one cooperates with the grace of God. It is a way to nudge creation ever closer to its intended design.

Work, of course, can be destructive. It can destroy the worker, it can destroy the family, and it can destroy the creation. The person who drearily goes to a job he or she detests can testify to the dehumanizing effect of work. The workaholic also shows the devastating potential of work. There are many examples, likewise, of where the pressures or consumption of work have destroyed marriages or have left children adrift. Similarly, one who has seen some of the ugliness wrought by the human hand can testify to the destructive force of human efforts in creation.

There is little sense in trying to tell people what type of work they should do. Should they be domestic parents? Should they seek a career that offers only a reasonable income and reasonable pressure? Should they follow their attraction for a job that thrusts them into the midst of intense demands? These are questions that people must answer for themselves in the concrete dynamics of their life as they expose themselves to the Christian call.

Somewhere along the line, however, married people, especially those with families, should ask themselves what impact their work is having on their life together. Part of that consideration will hopefully take into account the potentials that work offers the family. The monetary returns are obvious. Work, both in and out of the home, can also offer much to the personal enrichment of life.

The work ethic of life in which one had to be useful to be of value has come in for quite a beating over the last few decades. It did fail to appreciate the value of leisure time and recreation. It did fail to understand the importance of the quiet and the contemplative. However, in correcting the shortsightedness of the work ethic, the enriching value of work should not be dismissed.

E. Marriage and the Stewardship of Wealth

How a family uses the wealth at its disposal says much about the people involved in the marriage. It is no accident that many of the arguments in a marriage center around the use of, scarcity of, or drive for greater material goods. How people spend their money says much about the values that glue their lives together. Here are three household budgets. What do they say about the fabric of life in each family?

The Bergmans

After tax income: $20,000
Children: 2 teenage boys
         8-year-old girl

House payments	3,000
Upkeep, insurance, utilities on house	1,500
Car payments	2,400
Food	9,250
Clothes	1,150
Health insurance and medical bills	2,000
Household purchases	600
Charitable contributions	250

Transportation and car repair	450
Interest on loan	225
Recreation	500
Total	$21,325

The Princes

After tax income: $38,500
Children: none

House payments	7,000
Upkeep, insurance, utilities on house	2,100
Car payments	6,000
Food	13,300
Clothes	6,000
Health insurance and medical bills	1,700
Household purchases	3,000
Charitable contributions	350
Transportation and car repair	1,800
Interest	2,100
Recreation	5,800
Total	$49,150

The Burkes

After tax income: $73,000
Children: 8-year-old boy
         6-year-old girl

House payments	12,000
Upkeep, insurance, utilities on house	2,800
Car payments	4,800
Food	10,400
Clothes	3,400
Health insurance and medical bills	2,500
Household purchases	3,500
Charitable contributions	8,000
Transportation and car repair	1,800
Recreation	4,300
Total	$53,500

In looking at the three budgets, one should not have a difficult time identifying three typical types of families. In the first, the Bergmans, there is a family with a middle-class income from a full time and a part time job. The housing is moderate by today's prices. It does not represent extravagant accommodations in an impressively well-to-do neighborhood. The upkeep on the house does not present extravagant tastes. In fact the utility bill is inflated by leaky windows and inadequate insulation. The rest of the house's upkeep represents the higher costs of maintaining an older home. Actually, there is much that could be done to the house, but the funds are just not available.

The next item in the budget, the car payments, is the only sign of even a hint of extravagance for the Bergmans. They are in the final year of a four-year loan on one car and in the first year of a new four-year loan for the second car. They feel that they cannot do without two cars and hate to have older, less dependable ones.

The food bill represents about $178.00 a week. The only "fat" in the bill, as far as the Bergmans can see, besides that found in the hamburgers eaten twice a week, is the Friday night family restaurant binge that has been part of their tradition since their first son, Jeff, was two years old. Other items on the bill represent fairly basic expenses. The clothes are cut to a minimum. The parents especially keep things modest so that their more fashion conscious children can keep up with the Witherspoons and the Caseys. Health costs are dictated as are transportation costs. There is a family vacation which they feel is important. Theoretically it could be cut as could the charitable contributions, but they hate to have disappear from their lives all the elements of generosity to themselves and to others.

The problem, of course, is that their expenses outstrip their income. There is serious concern about the need for the wife to work full time. The older son could hold the fort at home after school until the parents returned from work. It might even do him good to assume the responsibility. However, the eight-year-old daughter does not want mommy to be gone when she gets home from school. The Bergmans feel, however, that the need for additional income must be faced sometime in the near future.

The Princes, while not embellished in royal grandeur, do have more economic assets at their disposal than do most married couples. Their $583.00 monthly house payments have not brought them extravagance. They live in a rather decent ranch in a suburb of a large metropolitan area. Again, any financial analyst brought in to help them live within their means might question two car payments. The American love affair with cars might have distorted their passions, but they see little room for compromise.

Their food bill is high compared to the Bergmans who feed five on four thousand dollars less per year. However, the Princes feel that their full time jobs entitle them to some pleasant dining experiences. Neither likes to cook, and they do not want to subject themselves to the crudities of McDonalds.

Other items that appear to be high in comparison to the Bergmans are, of course, their clothing bills, their household purchases, and their transportation. With both of them holding junior but professional jobs that hopefully will lead to climbing up the ladder, they find little room for cutting down their wardrobes.

The final household, the Burkes, are comfortable by today's standards. They live well but conservatively. They are a religious people who take the command to tithe literally. They give one tenth of their income to the church and face other charitable obligations with modest generosity. As financially conservative people, they have already begun to put away a considerable amount in various savings plans. If one compares their expenses in food, clothing, household purchases, as well as car payments with those of the Princes, it becomes obvious that their lifestyle is modest by the standards of present society.

The Christian Perspective

Christianity has always struggled with the proper use of material wealth. Spouses should not be surprised if it is a source of tension between them. The Bible is filled with warnings against the pull of material goods. Several passages in the gospels call for a renunciation of material wealth:

> Do not lay up for yourselves an earthly treasure. Moths and rust corrode; thieves break in and steal. Make it your practice instead to store up heavenly treasure, which neither moths nor rust corrodes nor thieves break in and steal. Remember, where your treasure is, there your heart is also (Mt 6:19–21).
>
> Another time a man came up to him and said, "Teacher, what good must I do to possess everlasting life?" He answered, "Why do you question me about what is good? There is One who is good. If you wish to enter into life, keep the commandments." . . . The young man said to him, "I have kept all these; what do I need to do further? Jesus told him, "If you seek perfection, go, sell your possessions, and give to the poor. You will then have treasure in heaven. Afterward, come back and follow me." Hearing these words, the young man went away sad, for his possessions were many.
>
> Jesus said to his disciples: "I assure you, only with difficulty will a rich man enter into the kingdom of God. I repeat what I said: it is easier for a camel to pass through a needle's eye than for a rich man to enter the kingdom of God" (Mt 19:16–24).

These passages give some idea just what a problem material goods present to the Christian call of life. The Christian message is a radical one. It demands that the believer cast aside all other concerns and pursue the work of God. Its most radical saints have usually abandoned the goods of this world as dangers to the call of Christ. Many like to have statues of Francis of Assisi in their manicured gardens. Francis, however, was not a precocious environmentalist. He encouraged all to abandon themselves to the providence of God and become like the birds of the air. He and the church of his day came into clear conflict over their attitudes toward wealth.

In a sense, when Christianity found itself in a dualistic setting, it was easier for it to embrace a radical renouncing of the world. The way of perfection, such as the life chosen by members of its religious orders, was to renounce the goods of this world as much as possible through personal vows of poverty. They were to remain in the world but not of the world.

The formula may sound fairly simple. But any awareness of the wealth of the medieval monasteries and churches would show that the solution was not that easy. A dualistic explanation would simply say that the goods of this world have an irresistible allurement. A viewpoint less hostile toward the goods of this world, however, could argue that there was a certain instinctive sense that worldly beauties are there for the benefit of all humans.

Today there is a more benign attitude toward the physical world. The beauties of material things are generally seen as reflective of the beauty of God. The body and the spirit are seen on a continuum where the spirit is shaped by the material world which serves as its base. But even with this more positive attitude toward the physical world, the problem of wealth will not go away. Many Christians have become consumers. They fail to stop and appreciate the delicate beauty that is around them.

Those who wish to preserve the beauty of the world see how the desire to own things drives people into a destructive pursuit. Material possessions can become an end in themselves rather than a means of sensitive enjoyment and developing awareness. The ferocious appetite of a consumer is never satisfied. It has a drive for more and more.

Many of the questions facing the modern marriage and family must take a blunt look at its materialism. Many of the key questions revolve around how much wealth a family needs and how to use it. There is no easy formula. There are many disturbing questions. Christians are keepers of their brothers and sisters. Every minor indulgence is done in face of the poverty that is around.

In looking at the Bergmans' budget, they are living a very modest lifestyle by the standards of their society. Where could they cut if they wished? Any cheaper housing would put them the other side of the poverty line. It would place their children in an environment where their chances in life would be clearly compromised. People are shaped by their environment. An environment where the gentle beauties of life are scarce tends to make people hard. Desperation brings a certain dehumanization.

Many people of quality, heart, and spirit grow up in the poverty pockets in our country. There is even a certain lesson about the goods of the world that can be learned from benign poverty. However, all this said, it is one thing to live by choice or even necessity in benign poverty. It is quite another to live in the midst of a people who desperately want more as they sit on the fringe of society and look at the goods others are enjoying. Such an enforced poverty embitters a large portion of the people who are forced to live in it.

The Bergmans' housing, then, takes a good portion of their income, especially when upkeep and insurance are figured into the expenses. It seems a necessary expense. Perhaps they could eat more modestly. Perhaps they could give up their vacation. But to what end? They could give more money to the less fortunate. They are aware of people starving in the Sudan. But such a radical cutback in the use of goods is only a good decision when all are comfortable with it. If either spouse feels resentment at living life on the edge, there will be bitterness instead of growth. Even if the children feel that they are left out of the "normal" and resent being where they are, then there could be more harm than good done to the growth of the family members. The family may be brought closer to resentment than love.

Spouses and their families are measured by their immediate environments. People living in Troy, Ohio, cannot measure themselves by the standard of living in a small village of a developing country. If a family can rise above the shortsightedness of their community, then let them do so. They should be aware, however, that prophets who voluntarily take up their role pay a price. The rewards can be great. The results can also be devastating.

Conformity also has its price. If the Bergmans decide to have both parents working, what will that mean for their family life? Will the bond and stability that they have achieved in their lives be hurt by the scampering to keep all their busy schedules together? Not necessarily. The positive and negative questions of two-career families have already been discussed. They should be aware, however, that achieving greater economic power has its price.

The Princes present a different set of circumstances. They are not living within their means. They should be able to do so. There are a few items that jump out in a budget in which expenditures exceed the income by more than ten thousand dollars. The car payments, the food, the clothing, the household purchases should be looked at carefully. The recreation budget is extravagant given their financial situation. Cruises can be enjoyable. Do they fit in where there is little chance of a balanced budget? Their charitable contributions amount to less than one percent of their after tax income. Even at that the only sizable sum came from their participation in the United Way fund in their offices. One could question whether those contributions were more career moves than acts of generosity.

In short, the Princes should step back and ask whether they are living beyond themselves in any way other than through their careers. Certainly they are living beyond their means. To continue to do so will entrap them in financial shackles. Their lifestyle is deeply embedded in their values. Their marriage faces some very difficult times ahead. It is not a question of one person going through the gut-wrenching search of how they are going to prioritize their life. Two people together must assess how they want to change. More basically they have to look at why they want to change.

The Burkes, who represent the upper eschelon of the middle class, offer a rather unusual mix. Their housing is comfortable but not extravagant. Their cars and clothes again are a bit better than most, but well within their means. The only area where they have been rather indulgent is in household purchases. Mr. Burke does have a weakness for machines. Mrs. Burke has an attraction to collectibles. But three and a half thousand dollars does not represent undisciplined spending.

The thing that makes the Burkes stand out is their serious commitment to sharing their wealth. There are not too many who contribute over ten percent of their income to charities. The Burkes do a little more. Still Mr. Burke feels guilty. He reads the passage of the rich man and feels that he has turned his back on the radical call to discipleship. He is torn as to what direction his life and his use of goods should take. He honestly feels, however, that he has not faced the question. His wife has only reluctantly agreed to the tithing and seems in little mood to entertain further giving. His sense of justice must extend to her and realize that her values and conscience must be respected. His children, who constantly compare their lives with the lifestyle of their friends, are interested in more and more. They have a hard time understanding what it means to share with each other. All the talk of sharing with the poor has limited impact. It is simply beyond them conceptually.

In a sense, Mr. Burke shows the dilemma of religion. When a person hears the call, nothing short of a radical dedication ever satisfies. The problem is that when one has committed his or her life to another and has a family, there are limits to the choices of life.

The struggle of these three families shows how the value question is intricately tied to the ways they use their material goods. How people use their wealth, especially where there is more than meets the minimum of life's needs, says much about what they have become and what they are reaching for. None of the three households, for example, showed any sense of using any of their wealth to further their education. The Princes and Burkes in particular had enough room to use their funds for educational means, but they did not feel the need to do so.

NOTES

1. Martin Buber, *I and Thou* (New York: Charles Scribner's Sons, 1958).

2. John Cheever, "The Sorrows of Gin," *The Housebreaker of Shady Hill and Other Stories* (New York: Harper and Brothers Publishers, 1958) p. 104.

3. Edwin H. Freidman, *Generation to Generation* (New York: Guilford Press, 1985) p. 42.

4. Eugene Kennedy, *Sexual Counseling* (New York: Continuum, 1977) p. 43.

5. Antoine de Saint Exupéry, *The Little Prince* (New York: Harcourt Brace Jovanovich, 1982).

6. Mary Jo Bane, *Here To Stay* (New York: Basic Books, Inc., 1976) p. 8.

7. Martine Segalen, *Historical Anthropology of the Family* (New York: Cambridge University Press, 1986).

8. From Gerard Calot, "La Baisse de la fécondité dupuis 15 ans," *Colloque national sur la démographie francaise,* June 1980, Institut National d'Etudes Démographiques. Noted in Segalen, p. 167.

9. Bishops' Committee for Pastoral Research and Practices, *Faithful to Each Other Forever* (Washington: United States Catholic Conference, 1988) p. 41.

10. Ibid., p. 45.

11. Ibid.

12. Ibid., p. 12.

13. Ibid.

14. John Paul II, *On the Family* (Washington: United States Catholic Conference, 1981) p. 27.

15. "Sex, Marriage, and Family," Social Statement of the Lutheran Church in America (New York: Board of Social Ministry) p. 5.

16. "Resolution on Abortion," General Board Reference. #8006.2:12/81 (Valley Forge: American Baptist Churches USA, 1981).

STUDY QUESTIONS

1. What are some of the reasons for marriage today? What is the primary one in the minds of most people today?

2. Is there a single reality called love?

3. What is necessary in a personal life before one can achieve any significant degree of intimacy with another?

4. What is meant by I-Thou, I-You, and I-It relationships? How frequently are they present in a marriage?

5. As people get older, how do the stages of marriage vary?

6. What basic lesson about human relationships must Christianity teach culture? What basic lesson has Christianity learned from the culture?

7. How has the modern attitude toward sex changed? What is the primary lesson about sexuality that the culture must learn?

8. Characterize the struggle of Christianity with the question of sex. What lesson does it have to teach people today?

9. What are some of the interpretations given to the patterns of child-bearing in this country?

10. What is the present Christian attitude about children? What are the present attitudes toward birth control and abortion? How do the two questions relate?

11. What is the Christian perspective on work developed in the text? How is it applied to domestic work and to one- or two-career families?

12. What does the family budget say about the values and vision of everyone in the household?

FURTHER STUDY

Bane, Mary Jo. *Here To Stay* (New York: Basic Books, 1976). Good study of the changing patterns in the modern family with the general thesis that marriage is not passing out of existence.

Bishops' Committee for Pastoral Research and Practices. *Faithful to Each Other Forever* (Washington: United States Catholic Conference, 1988). An inside look at how marriage is explained to church counselors.

Freidman, Edwin H. *Generation to Generation* (New York: Guilford Press,

1985). An excellent book that shows how the issues that arise in a marriage must be placed within the context of the family history.

Galvin, Kathleen M. and Bernard J. Brommel. *Family Communication* (Glenview, Illinois: Scott, Foresman and Company, 1986). Communication will not solve all problems, but it is a good starting point.

Jersild, Paul T. and Dale A. Johnson, eds. *Moral Issues and Christian Response* (New York: Holt, Rinehart and Winston, Inc., 1988). Many of the issues related to marriage are treated from the perspective of a Christian viewpoint.

Kosnik, Anthony, et al. *Human Sexuality: New Directions in American Catholic Thought* (New York: Paulist Press, 1977). A good study that shows modern Christians trying to confront issues of the day while remaining faithful to the tradition.

Levitan, Sar A. and Richard S. Belous. *What's Happening to the American Family?* (Baltimore: Johns Hopkins University Press, 1981). Shifts and trends in marriage and the American family.

Segalen, Martine. *Historical Anthropology of the Family* (New York: Cambridge University Press, 1986). Insightful interpretations of important statistical profiles.

9.

The Theology of Christian Marriage

———— ◇ ————

How do Christian churches view marriage today? If a person were to drive around the city, stop at a half dozen churches, and read the marriage ceremonies found in the various prayer books, would there indeed be a significant contrast? The answer is no. The Christian community has traveled through many settings, many cultures on its pilgrimage to discover the meaning of God's continual self-disclosure. In a sense it is a strange journey because there is no point in time when the journey is complete. It is a timeless pilgrimage.

A small but significant part of that journey is spent in trying to determine where marriage fits into the personal and the community search for God. As earlier chapters have shown, the Christian sense of marriage has varied through the centuries. Given this long, tortuous journey, it is somewhat surprising to find that today there is widespread agreement among the many denominations of Christian belief.

The ceremony of marriage is the ritual in which the church should speak its heart, and the different ceremonies parallel each other on almost every major point. Ceremony after ceremony clearly shows that marriage is not to be considered simply a human institution. It fits into God's design for creation. It will succeed only with God's blessing. It creates a bonding between the spouses. It constitutes a sacred commitment which should not be confused with a contemporary notion of romantic love. And finally, as a Christian commitment, it should be one that is made for a lifetime.

A. Marriage as Part of God's Plan

There are different phrases used to show that the churches consider marriage as part of God's plan. In the *Lutheran Book of Worship* one finds the following:

170

The Lord God in his goodness created us male and female, and by the gift of marriage founded human community in a joy that begins now and is brought to perfection in the life to come.

Because of sin, our age-old rebellion, the gladness of marriage can be overcast and the gift of the family can become a burden.

But because God, who established marriage, continues still to bless it with his abundant and ever-present support, we can be sustained in our weariness and have our joy restored.[1]

Similar sentiments are expressed by other churches. *The Book of Services* of the United Methodist Church affirms that the "covenant of marriage was established by God, who created us male and female for each other."[2] *The Book of Common Prayer* of the Episcopal Church asserts, "The bond and covenant of marriage was established by God in creation."[3]

This sense of marriage being grounded in a deeper reality is in direct contrast to the plastic worldview that characterizes much of modern thinking. People today are trained to ask two basic questions: What is to be achieved? How can reality be changed or restructured to facilitate the human design? There is little room in this secular way of thinking for an institution that is set in its basic structure and intent. But the Christian sense of marriage insists that marriage cannot change to accommodate human intention.

Christians speak of marriage being instituted by God as part of some overall plan or design for creation. They are implying that there are some givens which cannot be changed according to human whims or intention. In most Christian communities today, humans are seen as playing an important part in the immediate course of the world. But a religious sense of reality in general insists that people need to be guided in their decisions by the realization of something greater at the heart of the world. They must draw upon the fundamental rhythms of God's creation to keep their sensitivities alive. The human agenda is not the dominant one.

This sense of being part of a greater living whole is really the background for the Christian insistence that marriage in the church is not simply an agreement laid down by the mutual consent of the parties involved. If a couple chooses to marry in the midst of the Christian community, then they must understand what commitment means to a people who sense God active in creation.

A ceremony used in a local Church of the Nazarene captures how, for their community, marriage reaches its full potential only when placed within a larger calling: "May you have a great spiritual purpose in life and may you seek first the kingdom of God, that all other things may be yours."[4]

B. The Need for God's Blessing

The Christian community is ever aware that humans are in constant need of God's help. The traditional word used for this help is grace. At times the word is used to signify the life of God that has become part of the spirit and the makeup of each person. At times the word is used to capture the reality that God helps people directly. More often today the two uses are joined by the realization that the greatest help that a person can receive is to have the spirit of God at the heart of one's own being. This life of God which is a part of one's basic being gives the strength to accomplish much and to deal with much.

As a community which sees the human called to greatness, more specifically to life in the Spirit of God, the Christian community is ever conscious of how humans fall short in their effort. Marriage is no exception. Throughout the services there is a constant reminder that the marriage will more than likely fall on hard times. The exchange of vows brings the difficulties of life into perspective amidst the joy of the celebration. Again, the list of phrases vary. The point is clear: "in good times and in bad, in sickness and in health" (Catholic); "for better and for worse, for richer and for poorer, in sickness and in health" (Methodist); "in plenty and in want, in joy and in sorrow, in sickness and in health" (American Baptist).

Amidst this realistic view of life, however, the couple is constantly reminded that they can draw upon the strength of God to help them work through their difficulties. The blessing of God is constantly called down upon the couple. Early in the Catholic rite of marriage, the priest or deacon addresses the couple in the following way:

> My dear friends,
> you have come together in this church
> so that the Lord may seal and strengthen your love
> in the presence of the Church's minister and this community.
> Christ abundantly blesses this love.
> He has already consecrated you in baptism
> and now he enriches and strengthens you by a special sacrament
> so that you may assume the duties of marriage
> in mutual and lasting fidelity.[5]

The Methodist service makes the same connection between the blessing received in baptism and that now sought in marriage:

I ask you now in the presence of God and these people
to declare your intention
to enter into union with one another
through the grace of Jesus Christ,
who has called you into union with himself
through baptism.[6]

The service continues at a later point by confirming the need for
God to bless the union: "May God confirm your covenant and fill you
both with grace."[7] Likewise, at one point in a service used in the United
Church of Christ, the prayer is offered: "And since without your help we
cannot do anything as we ought, we pray you to enrich your servants
with your grace. . . ."[8]

One service used in a Baptist ceremony spells out more specifically
the help that is being sought:

As they enjoy the happiness that awaits them in their future, and as
they support each other for the facing of life's pain and sorrow, may
they look to you, the One Sure Foundation of life, to serve as their
guide and compass. Surround them with your presence; uphold their
life together. . . .[9]

This invocation of a greater power to help the couple as they commit themselves to each other is the key point of difference between a
Christian sense of marriage and its more secular form. Both can do well
in urging faithfulness and dedication to each other. Both can celebrate
the beauty of human love and sacrifice. However, the religious ceremony can more easily bring the larger drama into perspective. The secular sense of life is not finely tuned to that which lies beyond human cares
and intention. It does not easily move beyond the immediate.

By contrast, the religious sense of life in general and the Christian
faith tradition in particular have the sacred dimension to life as the
pivotal concern. There may be times when religion fails to appreciate the
sensitivities caught by the secular view. However, in capturing the journey of two people in a lifelong commitment, the Christian faith tradition
has much to offer.

C. Marriage Creates a Sacred Bond

The Methodist service speaks of the couple who "come to give
themselves to one another in this holy covenant."[10] The Episcopalian

opening prayer speaks of the "bond and covenant of marriage."[11] The Catholic ceremony at one point offers a blessing in the following terms: "Father, you have made the union of man and wife so holy a mystery that it symbolizes the marriage of Christ and his Church."[12]

This comparison between the bond of marriage and the bond between Christ and the church was first made in scripture by Paul. Themes from the gospels, epistles, and other scriptural sources are frequently used in Christian services. It is not surprising, then, to find a ceremony in a Church of the Nazarene picking up on the same image mentioned in the Catholic service. It speaks of "holy matrimony, which is an honorable estate, instituted of God, representing the mystical union that exists between Christ and His Church."[13]

It is clear, then, that all the services stress the bonding, the covenant, the sacred reality created by joining the two marriage partners together. If the marriage ceremony were the only reality of married life, there would seem to be few if any differences from church to church. There is, of course, life after the ceremony. There is the reality of insecurities, unruly appetites, jealousies, boredom, and bad breath. How do the churches view this bonding when the couple no longer feel that they can live together? How possible is it for the bond to be broken?

Obviously, in a society in which responsibly used statistics place the divorce rate somewhere in the forty percent range, the question is a dramatic reality. Churches are faced with de facto civil divorces and frequent requests for remarriage as families try to reconstitute themselves after the trauma of a breakup. Pastorally, there is a need to help the people who are hurting.

The churches are not uniform in their approach to the question of divorce and remarriage. Virtually all of them recognize the need for a civil divorce to allow a couple to live apart. There are times when a personal relationship simply has come to an end. There is, at times, no realistic hope of reviving the life of love and commitment together. The well-being of the partners demands that they be permitted to live separately.

To acknowledge the need for a civil separation, however, is one thing. To speak of a Christian remarriage is another. The solutions vary. All the churches feel the strain between the ideals expressed so beautifully in the ceremonies and the adjustments made in practice.

The Catholic Church is probably the most dramatic example of how a Christian community struggles with the question of divorce. It does not allow for divorce and remarriage in its practices. In its official positions developed on this point, it insists that the bond created in marriage cannot be broken by the couple or the church. There is a reality beyond human control. The reality of the marriage exists as long as both partners are alive.

Pastorally, the Catholic Church has responded to the hurt experienced in people's lives by looking at the initial marriage to make sure that the couple entered into a truly Christian marriage at the time of their commitment. Realistically, the church must admit that many who go through the ceremony do so out of social custom rather than religious fervor. If in the judgment of the church the couple did not truly understand or believe the Christian vision of marriage at the time of the wedding, then it declares that the unbreakable bond never did exist. An annulment is then given. It does not deny the love and commitment of the partners in the original marriage. It does not deny the existence of a civil marriage. It does not deny the legitimacy of the children. The annulment does, however, say that a fully Christian marriage did not exist because of the limited understanding or limited commitment of one or both of the partners.

For those who speak freely of supernatural realities that exist separate and distinct from the world of everyday life, it is easy to accept a bond separate and distinct from the actual experience of two people. People today, however, are more existential. They tend to be suspicious of positing reality outside of what is present in experience. A more existential mentality would insist that if the couple's life together is in fact dead, then the marriage is in fact terminated.

Often the discussion as to whether the marriage bond is breakable or not seems to pit against each other two different ways of looking at life. Both may have their limitations. Both bring out different dimensions of the faith experience. Perhaps what is needed is a completely different way of conceiving the question. However the issue is conceived, though, the Catholic Church still insists in its practice today that it does not have the power to declare an end to a marriage that was at its inception a true Christian marriage. Nevertheless, the issue does not go away quietly. There is considerable debate within the church. There is much discontent with the annulment process.

Pastorally the Catholic Church has made noticeable efforts to reach out to the divorced. This pastoral concern is clearly what prompted the following statement by Pope John Paul II:

> Together with the synod, I earnestly call upon pastors and the whole community of the faithful to help the divorced and with solicitous care to make sure that they do not consider themselves as separated from

the Church, for as baptized persons they can and indeed must share in its life.[14]

Obviously, the Catholic Church's idea of the marriage bond is quite different from that of other Christian communities. Some denominations take an intermediate step between the total ban on divorce and remarriage found in the Catholic Church and a relatively open acceptance of the reality of divorce and remarriage found in most mainstream Protestant churches. Using the literal words of scripture as a guide, they allow divorce and remarriage only for adultery. One local church, for example, has comprised a "Wedding Guide." It gives a whole list of practical information that a couple might have as they approach the church about their wedding. On the front page there is a very direct paragraph:

> If you have been divorced, you must have *biblical grounds* (i.e., adultery on the part of your former spouse(s). Otherwise the Church of the Nazarene forbids its ministers from performing such weddings.[15]

But even in the majority of mainstream Protestant churches which are fairly free in allowing for divorce and remarriage, the tension between the ideal and the reality is still present. These denominations try to balance the faith tradition's reservation about divorce with the need to minister to hurting people. Some traditions almost appear reluctant to allow the remarriage. Others seem to put aside the biblical caution and center on the realities faced by people and the need to take practical steps in helping them.

Prior to the recent merger of Lutheran churches, the American Lutheran Church offered this statement: "Divorce needs to be seen realistically as the breaking of an order of God, the public and legal recognition of an already broken marriage, the culmination of a process of alienation."[16] It then goes on to state that remarriage "is neither forbidden nor automatically endorsed by the church." However, one must realize that "the second marriage . . . may result in a new union which faithfully witnesses to God's purpose for marriage."[17]

An example of the second approach in which there is a more positive embrace of divorce if the needs of the situation demand it can be found in the United Methodist Church:

> The church recognizes that the covenantal relationship of marriage may be broken. If, after conscientious evaluation and counseling, divorce becomes the most healing solution available . . . the church must serve as a supportive community. . . .[18]

It then goes on to state:

> We recognize the right of divorced persons to remarry. God's forgiving and redemptive love allows us to become whole persons who are capable of beginning a new family, undergirded by faith in God.[19]

The Orthodox Church has a specific ceremony for second marriages. At one point a prayer offered by the priest clearly speaks of the indissolubility of marriage: "O eternal God, who hast brought into unity those who were sundered, and hast ordained for them an indissoluble bond of love. . . ."[20] The concluding prayer of the priest shows an uneasiness with the second marriage: "Cleanse thou the iniquities of thy servants; because they, being unable to bear the heat and burden of the day and the hot desires of the flesh, are now entering into the bond of a second marriage. . . ."[21]

D. A Lifetime Commitment

The divorce question shows two things. First, while the church speaks its heart in the marriage ritual, all the issues of church life are not addressed in the ceremony. Second, there are failures in life; and these failures demand that there must be some adaptation with the ideals of the Christian vision of life.

Christian ceremonies of marriage, however, are meant to celebrate the faith tradition and the excitement it has about people being called to participate in the life of God. The ideal in all the denominations is clearly a lifelong commitment. This is shown in ceremony after ceremony. Any union that is akin to the bonding of Christ and the church must be seen ideally as a lifetime commitment.

The Lutheran service gives a fairly standard version of the wedding vow:

> I take you . . .
> to be my *wife/husband* from this day forward
> to join with you and share all that is to come,
> and I promise to be faithful to you
> until death parts us.[22]

The phrasing in the other churches varies slightly. The intent is obviously the same. Some of the variations found are "as long as you both shall live" (Nazarene), "till death shall part us" (Church of Christ), "all the days of my life" (Catholic). The intents are the same.

The ceremony for the Presbyterian Church combines the promise of a lifetime commitment with the earlier theme that God's grace is absolutely necessary. It offers the following prayer:

> Eternal God: without your grace no promise is sure. Strengthen . . . [the spouses] with the gift of your Spirit, so they may fulfill the vows they have taken. Keep them faithful to each other and to you. Fill them with such love and joy that they may build a home where no one is a stranger. And guide them by your word to serve you all the days of their lives; through Jesus Christ our Lord, to whom be honor and glory forever and ever. Amen.[23]

CONCLUSION

In a way the prayer from the Presbyterian service is a good summary of the Christian view of marriage. It is an excited vision of a calling that the two partners can fulfill. It tries to energize its celebration with this excitement. However, there is the realistic human condition which often falls short of the calling. The failure is inevitable if people do not constantly place themselves in touch with the source of strength. All grace, all help ultimately is found in God whether the Spirit of God is specifically recognized as such or not.

NOTES

1. *Lutheran Book of Worship* (Minneapolis: Augsburg Publishing House, 1978) p. 203.
2. *The Book of Services* (Nashville: The United Publishing House, 1984) p. 64.
3. *The Book of Common Prayer* (New York: The Church Hymnal Corporation and The Seabury Press, 1977) p. 423.
4. "Wedding Guide," Parkview Church of the Nazarene, Dayton, Ohio.
5. *Marriage: Ritual and Pastoral Notes* (Ottawa: Canadian Conference of Catholic Bishops, 1979) p. 63.
6. *The Book of Service*, p. 64.
7. Ibid, p. 68.
8. "The Order for Marriage," David's United Church of Christ, Kettering, Ohio, p. 2.

9. "Wedding Ceremony," First Baptist Church of Dayton, Dayton, Ohio, p. 4.

10. *The Book of Service,* p. 64.

11. *Book of Common Prayer,* p. 423.

12. *Marriage,* p. 69.

13. "Wedding Guide."

14. John Paul II, *On the Family* (Washington: United States Catholic Conference, 1981) p. 82.

15. "Wedding Guide."

16. Standing Committee for the Office of Church in Society, "Teaching and Practice on Marriage and Divorce" (Minneapolis: The American Lutheran Church, 1981) p. 3.

17. Ibid., p. 4.

18. Family Life Committee: The United Methodist Church, *Family Life: A Resolution* (Nashville: Discipleship Resources, 1980) pp. 3–4.

19. Ibid., p. 4.

20. *Service Book of the Holy Orthodox-Catholic Apostolic Community,* Isabel Hapgood, trans., 4th edition (Brooklyn: Syrian Antiochian Orthodox Archdiocese, 1965) p. 303.

21. Ibid., p. 305.

22. *Lutheran Book of Worship,* p. 203.

23. *The Worshipbook* (Philadelphia: Westminster Press, 1970) p. 67.

STUDY QUESTIONS

1. What is the most significant difference between the Christian and secular view of marriage?

2. What is meant by the term grace? How does it fit into the Christian marriage ceremony?

3. What is the Catholic view of the bond that exists as a result of marriage? How does this view affect the practice of divorce and remarriage?

4. What is meant by an annulment?

5. What are some of the practices of divorce and remarriage found in Christian churches?

6. How does the notion of love developed in the Christian ceremony differ from a romantic view of marriage?

10.

Conclusion

———————— ◇ ————————

An evangelist in a non-western country is perhaps most aware of just how much religions are changed when they try to honor the images, the customs, and the sense of reality that govern a newly converted people. To speak of change is not to dismiss a religion as simply selling out to the demands of the day. Change still allows a faith community to embrace its founding or normative revelation. There still can be a tradition even if there is an adjustment.

The journey of Christian marriage captured in this book certainly shows that there have been significant changes in the way the Christian community considers marriage. Hopefully the reader does not draw the easiest conclusion that because the modern Christian attitude is so different from that found in the New Testament or so different from that found in the medieval period, there is in fact no Christian perspective on marriage. Change does not rule out substance. As the settings underwent significant changes, the tradition and heritage shed valuable and persistent light on the struggles of the day.

In each age the Christian tradition challenges its people to remember that they are made in the image of God. As such they are called beyond themselves to reach for the transcendent. They should discover the call to greatness, the grounding in the transcendent in themselves and in their spouse. How each community understands this call will vary. But the realization that one is called by God and loved by God is a moving experience that is bound to transform the sense of what commitment means in a marriage. Commitment in the Lord is different from an act done by two people who see little meaning in life beyond the meaning created by human endeavor.

This last phrase should not, of course, lead to a Christian triumphalism. The journey traced here should certainly impress upon a Christian the need for humility and the need for pilgrimage. Certainly the lessons of history teach the Christian how at times the church has had much to learn from others about marriage. The search for meaning and insight is poorly served when the journey of sincere people is measured on some rating scale. There is a common human journey that should be characterized by dialogue. Hopefully, the Christian community is faithful enough at any given time to offer others some insight from the mission of the Lord, but there are times when the community struggles so intensely that the work of the Lord is not easily discovered.

How marriage is seen in the tradition depends on many factors. When the presence of God, the sense of the transcendent, is intensely strong, everything does pale. It is difficult to focus too much on marriage and family. Likewise, when the community goes through periods in which the society is struggling for stability and there is a passion for order, there is usually not an ease with those dimensions of human life which make the human restless. Passions, appetites, emotions, feelings, and moods are seen as realities that must be harnessed. During times of unrest which may border on chaos, there is a need for control and order. In such a setting marriage will be valued for the stability it brings to society. Within marriage, however, there will be a caution toward discipline and self-control.

Likewise, in a period in which there is a degree of stability and a measure of luxury which considers the rights of each individual, marriage will be valued for what it adds to each individual life. There will be an emphasis on personal growth and development. A marriage that is stimulated by the drives so closely associated with the physical can be celebrated.

It would be foolish for Christians today to feel that they have the final answers. As Christianity makes its way into the future, it will probably take on a much more international flavor. The dominance of western culture in Christian thinking will more than likely be challenged as the church experiences its greatest growth in non-western countries. Future communities will look back hopefully with some understanding and perhaps some admiration at the struggles that have characterized the present church. They will not look back, however, simply with admiration.

The historical journey of marriage causes many today to shake their heads and wonder. Hopefully, there is enough depth to the historical study to allow the student also to admire and to empathize. It is important that Christians today realize that such skills are also going to be needed by future generations. It is important to realize the limitations of the present church so that the search will keep its intensity. One thing that the Christian vision cannot condone is a simple contentment. Contentment is Christianity's greatest enemy. It threatens to replace the upsetting presence of God with a blind embracing of a particular culture.

Issues—abortion, birth control, divorce, equality in marriage—that are so obvious to a yuppie in Connecticut are seen in a very different light by an African Christian. Religious meetings in such places as Rome that address the issues of marriage are no longer dominated by people from western countries. The largest contingent will more than likely be from Africa, Asia, or South America.

In other words the search is not complete. It continues. Fortunately, however, the search can anchor itself in the tradition. The community of the past and the guiding Spirit of the church can serve as a center of orientation. There is as much danger in ignoring the center of orientation as there is in trying to truncate the search.